A GORBALS LEGACY

To Jacqueline

A Gorbals Legacy

RALPH GLASSER

MAINSTREAM
PUBLISHING

EDINBURGH AND LONDON

First published in Great Britain in 2000 by
MAINSTREAM PUBLISHING COMPANY (EDINBURGH) LTD
7 Albany Street
Edinburgh EH1 3UG

ISBN 1 84018 336 5

A catalogue record for this book is available
from the British Library

Typeset in 11.5 on 16pt Van Dijck MT
Printed and bound in Great Britain by
Butler & Tanner Ltd, Frome and London

Contents

	Introduction	7
1	Ah Did You Once See Gorbals Plain?	15
2	Where the Lemon Trees Bloom	29
3	Mr Wolf and the Messiah	37
4	Poisoned Chalice	59
5	Curtains of Dust	81
6	Marooned	101
7	S. Giorgio's Bitter Fruits	113
8	The Esther Labyrinth	133
9	La Rue Plainte	157
10	Troy	175

Introduction

WHEN I STARTED WRITING *Growing up in the Gorbals* IN 1984, I asked myself why I found it so painful to set down the life of fifty years before, surely far enough in the past to have been fully digested. The answer should have been obvious; and perhaps it was, and I shrank from seeing it. Trying to relive history brought a flurry of voices, questions that had been beyond my powers to answer at the time. I began to see that that was the main motive for writing the book, to answer questions too long postponed, the perplexities of a very young man who knew so little of the human condition, forced to jettison a life whose claims upon him grew stronger in the very act of leaving it. I suspect I knew well enough that I had had fewer answers than I thought, especially about myself. Events alone were not enough. The springs of emotion must be sought far beneath the surface, their significance understood, whose mystery I had recoiled from at the time, when the passion to escape from the Gorbals was intense. Some of those old questions still challenged me. Who was I at that distant time? Who had I wanted to be? Hoffman – in Offenbach's opera *Tales from Hoffman* – and his lost reflection in the mirror comes to mind.

What I was escaping from was far from obvious – not simply squalor, hardship, constraints of time and place and personality and volition, days of labour in the factory. I had brushed aside many of the obvious discontents, and thought I was free of them for ever. There was a constant beckoning as from a distant drum that I had been aware of ever since consciousness began, indefinable but real. I had to answer it. The only way was escape. It seemed that the Gorbals was driving me away; but there was a contrary influence too, which I feared to understand. It would be many years before I saw that the presiding genius of the Gorbals, for its own inscrutable purpose, would never leave me. I see now that the Gorbals was not the malign influence I was driven to escape. I may have glimpsed the truth fleetingly along the way and wondered if I had seen it correctly. I needed to halt and confirm it again and again – which is why I entitled the first chapter of this book 'Ah did you once see Gorbals plain?', after the line in Browning's 'Memorabilia': 'Ah did you once see Shelley plain?', expressing the impulse to hold a fugitive vision steady and confirm its truth before the heart dares accept it.

In writing this coda to my Gorbals trilogy I see the journey in a stronger perspective than before, especially how the genius of the Gorbals kept me on course, ordained long before in the fevered dreaming of childhood.

When we think of childhood and early youth we may imagine that the visions of those days are too insubstantial and fugitive to inform the future – days when life was a stream of ghostly but powerful mirages whose meaning was always just out of reach, with only primitive instinct an uncertain guide through them. However, those years bequeath a legacy of passions and responses – the secret lineaments of identity – whose claims we never surrender.

That the genius of the Gorbals kept me on course was not easy to accept, yet it was always with me, a reference point for feelings, contrasts, a way of placing distance between the immediate experience and 'what the Gorbals would have thought . . .' – in the North

African desert, the bazaar in Pindi, the mountains of Calabria; a Faustian contract, the attendant spirit keeping a bargain that was always contingent – for I too had to keep faith, which I must have done unawares. The journey turned out differently from anything I had imagined. Returning to the Gorbals in imagination I reminded myself that my intuitive lodestone had not taken me far off course. Surprisingly, my Oxford scholarship essay with its set question: *'Has science increased human happiness?'* was also a firm reference point. My answer had been no – a verdict that remained unshaken throughout the journey and holds good today more than ever. For science read economic development, consumerism, faith in the Philosopher's Stone of high technology. Eliot's lines in 'Choruses' from *The Rock* put the matter incisively:

Where is the wisdom we have lost in knowledge?
Where is the knowledge we have lost in information?

When I wrote the essay in 1936, few wanted to recognise the urgency of the predicament set out in the above lines, except people who did not fear to be called cranks, such as Ezra Pound, many of them, alas, influenced by the poisonous charisma of the Strong Man. There was certainly confusion, a nervous twitch in the air, when I first ventured from the portals of the Gorbals, industrial power-house in decay — once the Second City of the Workshop of the World.

Now, even the physical Gorbals I knew has been destroyed, including much of the old street plan. When I go back it is almost impossible to identify the ground where former landmarks stood – Gorbals Cross and the darkly sculptured monument named after it, bearing under a clock the City of Glasgow arms and the motto 'Let Glasgow flourish by the preaching of the word', and stone benches on its walls where men in mufflers and cloth caps gathered on Sunday mornings to smoke and talk about the world; Cumberland

Street railway bridge with its broad arches, workshop caverns for upholsterers, metal workers, machine shops; and the old Main Street library. On a visit to Glasgow a few years ago, when journalists wanted to have me photographed at Gorbals Gross, we drove round fruitlessly till I realised that these Glasgow men were lost. I got out of the car, stood on an unknown pavement and, helped by a sighting on the steeple of a surviving church, led them to where Gorbals Cross had stood. I was photographed standing on a windy piece of wilderness, Gorbals Cross. The true Gorbals is in the heart. Its demons will probably stay there forever, waiting to receive *their* quittance.

Its condition expresses life's unwillingness to stand still while you try to achieve the changes it demands. Like many young people at the time I too must have wished the world would wait while I re-designed myself. I have written about Alec, who worked opposite me at the pressers' bench in the factory, who tried to persuade me to follow his quietism, accept life as I saw it, to him a natural view despite the terrible price it imposed. On his shoulders rested the weight of an ancient certainty, faith in the inevitability of fate, a courageous position to take in those days of confusion and unrest that were the 1930s. Days of resentment and doubt, of moral disgust, of forlorn attempts to deny the verdict that had come from the 1914–18 war – that the promises of progress were false. He knew – with Ecclesiastes – that time and chance were what life was about. You had to settle for that.

As I wrote in *Growing up in the Gorbals* I wished I could adopt his quietism, but the urge to move away – anywhere – would not leave me; and when I won the scholarship, and had the Oxford letter in my pocket, I was drawn on the rack. I see now that the choices were not as simple as that. As with Hoffman seeking his lost reflection, something must have made me turn away from my own. Looking back now, the Hoffman parallel can be made more compelling by means of a simple variation; could it be that he *did* see his reflection in the mirror but it was not the one he wanted to see! Hence his continued fury? That would mean that he was not at all sure *who* he was; he too wanted to escape from an old identity, old attachments, dependency, a directionless persona, and feared that the dream was impossible to fulfil. In the event his wild search did succeed, but at the very moment when romantic fulfilment came to seek him out, he was too drunk to claim it!

That could have been a parallel for me. In that state of mind the letter from Oxford was a way out, an excuse to postpone doubts about who I was, or should be. Let Fate decide. That is probably not a rare predicament but part of the given of living. As Ecclesiastes says: 'Time and chance happeneth to them all.' Who could wait for certainty?

The verdict of 1914–18 was hard to forget when I saw maimed ex-servicemen at street corners, when those streets thundered with protest – Wal Hannington and his National Unemployed Workers' Movement, hunger marchers, anti-Blackshirt skirmishes, cries of workers' rights, and that other cry, for 'human betterment', credo of yet another age of innocence that had created the Socialist Sunday School.

If Alec's settled quietism made him turn away from the miasma of disillusion, I had no such confidence. I was much younger and far less experienced. There *must* be a way forward! But I could not have said what 'forward' meant.

I did not know that the world changes before your eyes, and to think that you can keep pace with it, let alone move faster, is folly. The Gorbals must wait until I could face it squarely with a new persona. Many years would pass before I saw that the opposite would happen, that its culture, its values, were far more enduring than I had supposed; and their influence would accompany me wherever I went, and sweep aside private conceits.

I wonder if such thoughts of the self and the world were in Wordsworth's mind when he wrote:

I have learned
To look on nature, not as in the hour
Of thoughtless youth; but hearing often-times
The still, sad music of humanity

Impressions of change flow through the heart unchecked, and what you hoped you are 'making' of yourself, and what you wanted to be, assume a beguiling unity, usually false. The dream is impossible to fulfil – to redesign yourself while remaining the person you know, or think you know. The reality was that I carried the Gorbals with me on the journey unawares – adopting many avatars along the road, but always accompanied by the Gorbals, my Faustian familiar.

In these pages I show its steady influence. Central to my journey is the original scepticism of my scholarship essay. While science has improved many things, life expectancy for instance, the negative verdict is if anything stronger now; science has been crucial in making consumerism an end in itself, and instant gratification usurp permanent values. And 'happiness'? Who can now define that goal unequivocally? In place of an earlier confidence there is tell-tale fury, as when a radio audience rejected my provocative suggestion that there is no such thing as happiness, and that there was no better guide to the purpose of living than Ecclesiastes.

In Third World work I found the old Gorbals disillusion with the betrayals of progress repeated – but on a far greater scale of fury and tragedy. At conferences, when I argued that much of Western effort in taking 'development' to Third World countries amounted to transferring to them the human predicament of the developed West, I met an uneasy reluctance even to discuss the matter, followed by attempts to ignore the facts. My arguments did begin to influence policy in the direction of 'socially benign' development, but slowly.

Travel through time, as when I found S. Giorgio Albanese, a 'backward' community on the southern fringe of Europe still influenced by nineteenth-century faith in progress, took me back to the spirit of the Gorbals and to that of the dying socialist scholar Mr Lipchinsky – my communist friend Bernard's father – visionary believer in human improvement. Where had my journey begun, I asked myself. Had it begun at all?

Retracing my steps in this book, I saw that the journey had indeed begun earlier than I had thought – in childhood, where fury and impatience prepare for the future. There must have been many signs of what had been stored up. One of them must surely have been my nearly fatal confrontation with nature at the Inversnaid Falls described in Chapter One, when life and death were too nicely balanced. It might have been a dramatic warning to myself, acciden-tally on purpose, that hope and confidence were not enough in facing life, long before I read Wordsworth's revelation of the 'sad music of humanity'.

I had never escaped from the Gorbals. I see now that its genius had sent me on a quest for something too fugitive to be the stuff of cold logic, an identity constantly explored but never accepted until I stood at Schliemann's Trench on the hill of windy Troy.

ONE

Ah Did You Once See Gorbals Plain?

WHEN DID THE NEW QUESTIONING BEGIN, AND WHAT PROMPTED it? It started some years after *Growing up in the Gorbals* appeared – small hints, fugitive recollections of comments on life from Alec or Meyer or Father – many voices – long ago; and I paused in the middle of other things and wondered at the reason for the intrusion, what it was that my inner self wanted me to know. Meyer was an especially poignant memory, who had fought the 'debt enforcers' and lost. Each time the voices were more insistent, telling me to look beyond the ghosts that had surfaced in that book. Their promptings must have begun long before, perhaps when Bernard had uttered one of those statements, superficially trite but expressing spiritual pain, that echo in the mind long afterwards: 'We are none of us where we wanted to be' – and demons long forgotten demanded appeasement.

I saw that although I had been drawn back into the Gorbals while writing that book, I had needed to keep it at a certain emotional distance to write it at all – hard to believe when I had thought I would never feel so deeply about the Gorbals again. Yet there must have been 'something far more deeply interfused' that demanded acceptance; and now, years later, the demons tell me to go back to emotional depths I had tried to ignore. I saw that I had tried to hold a certain essence of the Gorbals at arm's length for half a lifetime – and that to have done so had been not only foolish but futile. The Gorbals world view refused to fade away. In a fashion not yet understood, I needed to join it to my own at last. Trying to escape its influence had been natural at the time; I must discover why I now needed to possess it wholly.

Long ago, when that ragged boy had enrolled in Glasgow University evening classes, had he secretly hoped for a mysterious deliverance? Not consciously; but I must have determined, with a kind of magical possession, to entice the Fates to intervene – how, in what way, and why should they? I could not have said. A decision there must have been; how had I come to it?

Thinking back further and further, I remembered an event that I must have tried hard *not* to recall, when the emotional fuse must have been lit, though the train must have been laid long before – a day when I came within an ace of death. As sometimes happens with events too traumatic for 'normal' understanding – often, as this one was, of one's own unthinking devising – the spirit refuses to give them house room and takes refuge in forgetfulness.

I was about sixteen, and had stayed the night at a youth hostel near Loch Lomond one Hogmanay. People I had met at the hostel suggested I join them the following day to go to another hostel on the far side of Ben Lomond. I said I would, but that instead of accompanying them on the climb to the shoulder of the mountain and down the other side, I would walk round its base. I remembered wondering why they looked at me in surprise.

Why I had made this decision I had no idea. There was one reason, influential for a young person, that I was not as well equipped as these newly made friends; I lacked proper boots and good outdoor clothing. In retrospect there must have been something for which I needed solitude, and the remoteness of nature, to settle with myself.

It would be a year before I saved enough to buy hobnailed boots to replace the old shoes I wore, and an army surplus rain-cape that doubled as a ground sheet. Even so, going up over the shoulder would not have been difficult, hardly a climb at all, for there was a clear path. I was reasonably experienced, and had grown to love being on mountains, a world with whose voices I was in tune, far from the Gorbals and its enchainment. This makes that day stranger still in retrospect, for I behaved with less than the usual respect for the conditions. I learnt years later that to do so signals a hidden concern so important, yet so deep, that it chooses a climacteric way of forcing the reluctant spirit to face it squarely.

Contributing to that decision may have been something that happened the previous evening when there had been a special Hogmanay supper at the hostel. We were given slices of cake and told to be careful biting into it because it contained 'prizes' – little figures or coins. For the first time in my life I won something – a silver threepenny piece, the envy of all the others, for a silver coin was a rare prize. I took this as an omen – for what I had no idea, but I was at an age for omens. They were important; they had to be. I must look for a change in my life. It was a duty. And the next day was the first day of a new year.

Perhaps I had decided to test the omen the next day by starting off late in the forenoon, crucial as it turned out.

The day was grey with black cloud hanging low, threatening rain. I walked down the slope to the ferry, a large rowing boat, for the crossing to Rowardennan on the far side of the loch, at that point about a mile across. The ferryman was a sturdy white-haired man with the wind-cured features of one who lived close to nature. He told me it was his birthday, and that he was eighty. He too, when I said I was going to walk round the base of Ben Lomond, first of all to Inversnaid, about six miles along the loch, along a track I had never tried before, looked at the lowering sky and then searchingly at me and at my worn shoes. He did not comment. I paid him the fare of threepence, and sat in the stern while he pulled with short, steady strokes on the still water, slowly as it seemed to me, saying nothing, looking straight over my head at the sky, the rhythmic strokes hypnotic, the loch sliding past with a soft, rustling sound against the timbers, dreamlike. I almost wished I could stay on the boat for ever. I did not know that it would not be long before I wished I had.

At the far side of the loch, as I clambered on to a low wooden jetty, the ferryman said: 'It's going to rain soon, and it will last all day.' He looked along the jetty to see if anyone wanted to cross for his return journey, and, seeing no one, pulled away.

He was right. Heavy rain began, of a steady kind that I knew could well last all day. I shrugged the thought away. I was full of the good omen of the silver threepenny piece, and still in the dream state created by the ferryman's slow, rhythmic oars; and dreamed that one day I would lift the thrall of the Gorbals – though how I could achieve it I had no idea, or *what* could free me of it, something I had never dared consider seriously before. The sense of freedom in this lonely world of mountain and loch, however harsh the conditions, was magical – neither friendly nor hostile but with the potential to be either; and possessing a further element, an aloofness like that of the stars, with an impending message never quite grasped, a whisper that might bring illumination at any time. And you must be attuned to it at every moment, like that ferryman was, who had listened all his life.

I was not even sure what 'freedom' could mean. The nearest I came to understanding it was to be where I was, in spite of the steady rain, on this mountain slope where I understood what was required of me – as I thought – as opposed to the Gorbals with its implacable weight. This was the first time I had ever thought of myself as a person with my own judgment of the world, though that nascent sense was shot through with fear of the unknown – aware of a mystic distance between where I stood in the sodden remains of bracken, with the leaden sky hanging close above my head, and with a new-found vision of the Gorbals at a distance from me. That hint of a new knowledge of myself was exhilarating and frightening.

About an hour later – I had no watch – trudging along an overgrown track that frequently lost itself among trees and shrubbery on the slopes rising from the loch, the rain had soaked me so completely that not an inch of me was dry, and my wet feet squelched through thick layers of old fallen leaves, or sank into sodden earth. The loch was partly hidden in rain mist, the far shore now invisible, and I wished I had taken the path over the shoulder of the mountain, at least for company – New Year's Day was considered a good day for 'crossing the Ben'. I would not have had the rain dripping down from the trees as well as from the sky. I stopped and looked back and thought of retracing my steps, but I was sure, wrongly as I was to discover, that I had gone beyond the halfway distance.

I was deep in thoughts of where I was in what seemed a new life opening up, rambling visions of the unknown future – in retrospect forewarnings of distant maturity. I was already tired from walking heavy-footed through wet earth, catching my feet in fallen branches concealing puddles where recent snow had melted – feeling cold in spite of the activity, and not thinking clearly.

It was dawning on me that I had been foolish to attempt this walk. At the end of this track were falls where the River Snaid tumbled into the loch, and there was a bridge marked on my map at the falls themselves, that led on to the road on the far side, where there was a small hotel – and where, with luck, I could ask for shelter in an outhouse. Unusually, for I was careful about details, I had not troubled to find out the exact position of the bridge, which I could easily have done at the hostel before leaving, or even from the ferryman. Yes, I *had* left far too late, underestimating the time needed in these conditions. Stopping under a dripping tree to munch a sandwich, I saw that there could at best be two hours of real daylight left, probably less under the low-lying cloud.

Dimly I began to suspect that I had overestimated the distance I had covered; I must be nearer the starting point, Rowardennan, than I had thought, and had made the wrong decision in carrying on. Yes, I should have turned back. Later, I admitted to myself, it was plain that I had chosen – yes, that was the word – to go against what I must instinctively have known.

And so I carried on, with brief stops as I grew more tired and cold. Soon my sandwiches were eaten, and the rain was making me feel colder still and stiff. Foolishly I did not think of getting my paraffin stove out to make tea with water from one of the many burns trickling down the slopes, which might have revived me – forgetting outdoor lore gathered from other wanderers, older, more experienced, met on mountain 'drum-ups' or in youth hostels at night beside the stove. Always keep heat going, and be alert for signs of mental fatigue, which slowed everything one did, piled mistakes one on top of the other, cumulatively dragging one down.

Suddenly, I woke from the dream state. The afternoon had slipped away. It would soon be quite dark. I listened for the sound of the Inversnaid Falls but there was only the steady patter and rustle of the rain. The trees were ghost-like, the loch invisible. I plodded on as in a nightmare when one's steps continue but no movement happens. Earth and sky and trees were one wet and cold continuum, with blackness everywhere. At last I heard a faint, low-pitched vibrating sound like distant thunder; it must be the falls. My spirits lifted; the bridge must be near. I would soon be crossing it. Of course it was now too late to think of continuing the walk round the base of the mountain. I would have to beg for shelter in a barn or shed at the inn. The thought of being out of the cold rain was like a balm.

In the intense darkness I began to wonder where I would find the bridge, with nothing to tell me whether to look for it to the right, upstream, or to the left, towards the loch.

Soon the falls sounded close, though muffled by the rain and the mist. My legs were so tired and cold that moving them at all was like lifting heavy blocks of stone unconnected with me. And still the falls, though they could now be separated from me only by a curtain of trees and bushes, came no nearer. At last the clamour and rush of tumbling water seemed so close that they might have been directly under my feet, and with a chill shock I realised that this was almost literally true. Instinct made me halt, and not a moment too soon. I stood on a steep, soft bank of soaked earth in which my feet sank and slipped, threatening to send me into the angry turbulence below. I lifted my eyes, and there were lights only a stone's throw away, on the other side of a narrow gorge that was like a cleft made by a titanic axe.

There was no sign of a bridge. The lights of the inn were not near enough, or not bright enough, to reveal anything but dark shapes of trees and shrubs on either side of where I stood, and down in the cleft at my feet the rumbling maelstrom of the falls.

So steep was the bank that I feared to go down any further lest I lose my footing altogether. In any case, the bridge could not be down there. Now, I did something sensible for the first time that day – unthinkingly, but it saved my life. To have wandered along the side of the gorge in the pitch darkness looking for the bridge would have been suicidal – one false step, one stumble or slip or loss of balance on the sodden slope, would have sent me into the falls. I sat down in the wetness – I was soaked through so that made no difference, got out my Primus stove, reached around me for some fallen twigs and branches, all of them wet, splashed paraffin on them and managed to light a match. Soon there was a small, yellow burst of flame, in which I dried additional sticks to add to the fire. I decided to move no further, thinking – though it was hardly clear thought – that I might make tea and get warm. Tea was impossible, for I dare not try to find a safe stretch of the river upstream to get water and it would take time to fill a mug with rain water. I was too exhausted to think of anything except getting warm, though of course there was no possibility of getting dry, there being no shelter whatever. Nor did it occur to me that I might not survive the night, cold, wet, tired, and now hungry. In a dream state, I held my hands over the flames, and wondered why I had got myself into this predicament. But I was too tired to think, except of the warmth creeping back into my hands.

It struck me that I really did not care what happened, a feeling I could not remember ever having had before. Nor did it seem bizarre. No, I did not care. It seemed that I had come all this way to reach this summing up. Later, looking back, I saw this whole experience as a self-imposed test – a test to destruction. I was at an *ultima Thule* of endurance, in this dark corner of the world, whence I could go no further, and there was no way back. And this thought clearly applied to the Gorbals – of which my predicament, trapped on the wrong side of the falls, was a direct parallel. Unless – unless what? Unless I broke free in some way as yet unknown.

Strange that I had room in my thoughts for that, but perhaps the warmth returning to my hands revived the resilience of youth.

I compressed myself into that small compass that nature induces to conserve body warmth, while the roar of the falls hammered home the thought that there on the other side of the cleft was light and warmth, far beyond my reach.

Suddenly I was aware of a new set of sounds and new lights – men's voices shouting on that far side, and the beams of several powerful torches swinging from side to side. The torches moved along the far bank till they were directly opposite where I crouched over my fire. The shouts, impossible to understand over the noise of the falls, rose higher and higher. Then the torches began to swing purposefully on to me and then down to a spot on the bank below me a few yards to my right – back and forth, back and forth. Could they be signalling to me to go to where the bridge must be, invisible from where I sat? I put my arms through the straps of my pack, and bent low to be able to touch the sloping bank to steady myself in the sodden earth and edged towards the spot – and then I saw that the torches were not pointed at any bridge, but at two six-inch planks stretched side by side between two rocks jutting out from the earth on either side of the gorge directly above where the first cascade of the falls began, which the torch beams revealed as a boiling white cauldron. Now the torches waved at me with an impatience that coldly transmitted itself to me, and then at the two planks, urgently now. There was no other way.

I knew that if I tried to walk upright across those two planks I would stagger and fall into that crucible of leaping water below me. There was no time to think. I *must* cross – somehow. I slid down, bottom in the loose earth, till my feet touched the nearside rock overhanging the plunging foam, on which the planks were anchored. I bent down, balanced my pack centrally on my back, hands stretched out till fingertips met the planks in front of my feet, and focused my eyes on the rough surface of the planks illuminated by the torchlight, though it was impossible not to see that churned up water not many feet below me, and began to inch my way across. And again and again there resounded in my mind the words – 'I don't care!'

Which might have been the influence that saved me. I did not see how far I had gone or had to go, only that I moved forward, inch by inch, on those planks only fractionally wider than my sodden shoes, and my pack did not slip, and again and again I shouted into the noise and the darkness: 'I don't care!'

The next thing I knew, the planks came to an end on the rock on the far side, held by an iron bar across them, and the torches blinding me, and hands gripped my arms and held me steady, and I realised that the man who held me was being held in turn by a chain of men behind him on the steep bank. They hauled me up and on to the road. And the feeling of my numb feet on the asphalt was like a miracle, as if I had long given up the thought that I would ever experience that solidity again.

They must have carried me the short distance to the inn, for I have no memory of walking there. Once inside, a woman's voice exclaimed: 'He's only a boy!'

I was incoherent, shivering violently. With the tension of crossing those two narrow planks released, I was in no state for speech of any kind. I can remember uttering the words 'Shelter – please, please. Out of the rain', and the woman telling the men to carry me to a room beside the kitchen, and being lifted like a stretcher case but without the stretcher, into a room nearby, my clothes, so wet that they clung to my skin, being pulled off, and a warm blanket wrapped round me, and set down at a table. Someone gave me a glass and told me to drink the contents, a honey-coloured liquid. I had never tasted whisky before, and began to choke. The woman stroked the back of my neck and made soothing noises, and I drained the glass, and my insides were warmed and my head tingled. Then a plate of thick porridge appeared in front of me, with steam rising from it, and I ate and felt the heat go down through me like a poultice reassuringly applied.

What was happening slipped in and out of consciousness, like lantern slides slotting images in and out. I was lifted again and carried along a corridor and inserted in a bed where a stone hot water bottle had been placed, and warm crisp sheets tucked under my chin, and thick blankets completing the cocoon of soporific comfort, silently administered, a completeness of care and concern never before experienced. The last words I heard were the woman's, saying to someone: 'There now – you can hang his clothes up by the boiler. He's young and looks strong enough. He should be right as rain in the morning. What a miracle he thought of lighting that fire! And that we saw it in time – aye, a miracle!'

I woke up and it was daylight, and I felt I had only that moment gone to sleep, but I must have slept well into the morning. The rain was still coming down, but the sky was brightening. It seemed that my mind had not moved since the middle of my transit of the planks, and that I was halted there still, so near the hurtling cascade, feeling that the white masses of water reached up to tear me down and engulf me if I did not move – but I could move no further.

Getting out of bed, I heard the falls beyond the window and went over to look out. The sun had come out. The slopes of Ben Lomond looked green and fresh. A new world.

I shivered, and realised I had not a stitch on. I must have made a sound, for the door opened, and the woman I had seen the evening before came in. She held a green woollen dressing-gown spread out before her ready for me to put on, half-concealing her face: 'Put this on you. A good morning to you, laddie. I know you slept well. The good Lord looked after you. There you are.'

I took the dressing-gown from her and she turned slightly away, and I did too, as I put it on, the first I had ever worn.

Seeing me fumble with the unfamiliar cord, she stood behind me and tied it for me: 'There you are. Now come into the kitchen and have some breakfast.'

I said: 'No, please. Just a drop of hot milk. I'll pay you . . .'

She interrupted: 'I'll not hear of it. It's not given to us to save a life every day. And a bit of Christian charity is a good thing to do, especially on New Year's Day.' She put her fingers over her lips in uncertainty, then went on: 'It was God's mercy to let us save you and that's a fact. After what you went though! I will not hear of you paying a single penny. Come along to the kitchen and sit down at the table. And then your clothes will be dry for you.'

I nodded, amazed, still wondering how I could pay. Then as she turned away again, she pointed to the bedside table: 'There's your things – we had to empty the pockets to hang your clothes up to dry.' And went out.

There were the coins, five shillings and some coppers – a small fortune saved for this holiday; and the matches in their tin box, my map, and a notebook and pencil. There, in fragments, lay my total self – nothing more – and with it I must conquer the new world I had found; for that was what it seemed like. That thought stopped me in my tracks. The experience had confirmed something for me. Somehow I *was* going to escape the Gorbals. How, I had no idea; a bridge of a different kind that I must find.

I ate breakfast alone at a long, scrubbed table in the kitchen, while the house echoed with the noises of domestic comings and goings. The woman came in from time to time to set more food before me, and I was a little abashed at eating so much. When I was nearly finished, she told me my clothes were dry and they had put them in the room where I had slept. 'I hope,' she said, 'you will come back one day and tell us how you are. Don't forget that we are part of one another when something like this happens.'

Her words confirmed a feeling I had had as I sat there, that I had emerged from an important rite of passage – one that I would not identify till much later, a reminder, or a warning, of approaching manhood – of many things as yet unknowable. I knew only that the experience had changed me – and perhaps that had happened to them too, that all experience changed you.

It was strange, too, that they had not asked what had brought me to the falls in the dark, not knowing where the bridge was. I sensed that they too had to digest the experience.

When I was dressed, I offered once again to give the woman some money. She treated the suggestion with a kind of dismay, as if I committed sacrilege. We were joined together by the experience, she seemed to say, and one day it might be *their* turn. That raised me to their level – to know that experience was not all one way.

As I walked along the road, my shoes felt hard from having been dried near a fire, the uppers cracked rather more than they had been before. With that sensation I was seized by a crippling terror of the crossing of the falls, as if it returned to compensate for not having defeated me at the time, and I wondered how I had managed to keep my balance while out-staring the white cauldron under my feet. The answer came, but it was unbelievable. I had shouted: 'I don't care!' – and must have meant it.

Could that be true? Yes. It must have been. The fierce tenor of the words came back. I stopped and stared at the revived green of the newly awakened world, dangerous if you treated it with indifference as I had done the day before. And I knew that I could never do the like again. Indifference would always bring Nemesis. I did care. I cared too much. And from now on I must find a way of taking charge of my destiny, though what that meant I could not have said. Here on this empty road, the inn now out of sight and the falls a distant murmur, the Gorbals was suddenly no longer overwhelming – a way of meeting it on something like level terms *was* possible. That was surely the aim – and I felt that a way was opening up. To know it, to see it steadily, as the ferryman had seen the world. The question was how? Somewhere in the future the answer must be waiting. I had to believe that.

I did go back, but as with so many aspects of youth, experience had dulled the immediate memory – perhaps the only way of living with it – and it was not till more than ten years later that I did so. The woman had gone, and none knew who it was I remembered. Nor had anyone heard of the incident. It felt as if part of me was in limbo for ever. I walked away again along that silent road as on that morning after my rescue, the world changed and yet not changed at all, the mountain green and glowing, the falls and their tumult receding once more, and sadness emphasising the echo of each step I took.

TWO

Where the Lemon Trees Bloom

THE EXPERIENCE BURIED ITSELF ONCE MORE IN FORGETFULNESS, but its influence remained, projected far into the future – the knowledge that the Gorbals world view was too powerful to oppose or to live with. And now, decades after I had left, it wielded a weight of certainty too strong for me. That 'reason' for flight – the true reason – was submerged under something else, a view I knew to be false but did not know why, the Utopian talk of the older people round me, in the Workers' Circle, or at Gorbals Cross, or Bernard's visionary father dying as he proclaimed that a new awakening was imminent. A few determined thrusts of the collective will would sweep away all obstacles to happiness. Looking back many years after I had left, I saw this talk as a last expression of nineteenth-century faith in human perfectibility – a sunset vision among many others that people clung to in the Gorbals of that time. The other, deeper reason for flight, to be free of the weight of the Gorbals world view altogether, would be hidden for many years, together with another even more disturbing: the knowledge that I could not live without it.

A lifetime later, not long after *Growing up in the Gorbals* appeared, these thoughts surfaced when I was invited to present a phone-in programme on radio, on a provocative topic of my own choice. Rather to my surprise I chose: 'There is no such thing as happiness!' – a teasing conceit I told myself. Then I saw that it expressed a view of the world that had worried me through childhood and as a young man – as well as intermittently since – and that it must have influenced my response to the question set for the Oxford scholarship essay: 'Has science increased human happiness?'

Happiness was not self-evidently part of life, I suggested, accessible to everyone, but a dream whose realisation was tantalisingly out of reach. Poetry and song and legend presented it as a state of serene existence in which distress and disappointment and deprivation either did not exist or vanished as soon as they appeared, or when looked at in a certain way. In the essay I had argued 'no' to the question asked. If happiness was a natural feature of the human condition, why did people talk of it as if only a poor substitute was ever attainable – and even *that* was evanescent, never to be grasped whole? If, after thousands of years of thought and dream and curiosity and experiment, questions about the nature and attainment of happiness still begged for answers, was it sensible to ask them at all?

I began the programme with Ecclesiastes, The Preacher – 9:11:

> I returned, and saw under the sun, that the race is not
> to the swift, nor the battle to the strong, neither yet
> bread to the wise, nor yet riches to men of understand-
> ing, nor yet favour to men of skill; but time and chance
> happeneth to them all.

You took the rough with the smooth and did the best you could with your life. What was 'best'? You had to decide that for yourself. The phrase 'time and chance' was a way of referring to the Divine Will, always unknowable. What you hoped for might be the 'wrong' things – dangerous or unattainable choices – but time and chance gave you few clues, except the gleanings of experience, and little or no scope for changing course. To hope for a state of absence of doubt, disquiet, uncertainty, was futile. You did what you could with life as you found it. In effect The Preacher said that the best recipe for living was to grit your teeth and keep going. He makes no mention of happiness, only of certain types of worldly fulfilment, metaphors for hope and reward.

Did anyone know what happiness was? And among those who claimed they did, was there unanimity? It seemed not. Did the word simply mean an absence of unfulfilled desires? The *Shorter Oxford Dictionary* says happiness is 'The state of pleasurable content of mind, which results from success or the attainment of what is considered good' – with the date reference 1592. 'Good' begs many questions. Does it refer to a moral state or a sensual one? Must other people approve? Is 'pleasurable content of mind' nothing more than feeling pleased with oneself whatever the reason? And if so for how long? Or does duration not enter into it? That can hardly be so. In history, literature, folklore, duration is important. The 'pleasurable content of mind' must be more than a passing sensation, like drinking champagne or eating a good dinner. Nor is it something one can plan to achieve, for The Preacher emphasises *chance*, the luck of the draw. While the desire to achieve it is natural, he warns against thinking of its pursuit as the *purpose* and aim of living.

Could happiness signify a never-never-land of perfection that only poets and other dreamers could see? Take Goethe, for example:

> *Know you that land where the lemon trees bloom?*
> *In the dark foliage the gold oranges glow;*
> *Where a wind ever soft from the blue heaven blows,*
> *The myrtle is still and the laurel stands tall – do you*
> * know it well?*
> *There, there I would go, O my beloved, with thee!*

To ask whether Goethe is talking about a 'real' place or a state of mind is irrelevant. The poetic imagination conjures its own romantic reality to compel the spirit.

Could it be, as Machiavelli might have proposed for the individual's existence as he did for that of his Prince, that the idea of happiness is simply a convenient myth, best not examined closely, a carrot to keep one pressing onwards? Never mind whether you reach the fancied goal or not – or even if it exists! Without that necessary myth, life would be too wearisome to endure. Alas, most of us prefer to turn away from The Preacher's parameters for living; we cling instead to myths handed down as comforters from the past.

Excited telephone calls to the studio showed that I had touched painful sensitivities. I should not have been amazed at the fury, even fear, that erupted. Few wanted to pause and consider The Preacher's view of life as hearty pragmatism, distillation of age-old experience. God could surely not be so unfair to those He had created as to give them no surer reward or guidance. How could I be so arrogant as to cast doubt on the emotional props people clung to, by questioning beliefs that had comforted a thousand generations?

A few voices conceded that I had touched doubts they already had. If we cannot believe in happiness as the prize of living, how shall we decide *what* to try for? How are we to measure success or failure, for surely we must do that?

Probably all deliberation in public, in whatever medium – including the written word – is self-indulgence. I must have needed to review my journey yet again and have some of its lessons reflected back to me in these voices. That thought was later confirmed in 'hate' letters from members of the unseen audience: 'If that is what you think, why bother us with it? It's *your* problem, and you deserve it. Leave us in peace to believe in happiness if we want to, in whatever form we think of it. What *we* believe is none of your business.'

Voices from childhood in the Gorbals returned, seeming to

paraphrase The Preacher: 'Expect nothing and you will not be disappointed!' – bitter wisdom I must have absorbed long before I understood it. I could hardly believe that I was being drawn back to consider the Gorbals afresh.

I thought I had forgotten the essay question and my reply to it, but now I saw that it had continued to occupy my thoughts through the years. My 'no' to it has remained my view, but I was beginning to understand how strongly that springtime thinking had conditioned my journey later on. In youthful vigour I had opposed the received view of those 1930s days – that progress, with science as its handmaiden, would solve the human predicament. That view had sent progress on quite the wrong path. What people *thought* was their quest for happiness was often something shallower – a modish, acquisitive pursuit of comfort and display – while beneath it lurked the suspicion that what they strove to grasp was the shadow of another, truer fulfilment, never properly defined. When I was writing the essay – in late adolescence – I thought I knew how to define happiness. Surely it was the state of being complete? That thought had stopped me in my tracks. I had only an indistinct vision of what I meant by 'complete' – how could anyone be complete? And how did we know when we *were*?

It seemed to be a mysterious state read about but not experienced. Or perhaps I *had* experienced it without recognising it, in moments of solitary communion with nature in the mountains, in crisp winter silence in the snow; a feeling of simplicity and perfection prompted by a serene blue gleam in the icy shadows on the high slopes, or pale sunbeams in sombre gullies as dusk drew near. Or when tramping down steeply to the flat land after a winter's day on the high ridges, the ground cold and tumbled, the short herbage rustling in the darkening breeze; and far below my jolted knees the strip of grey road rising towards me with every step, a vandal intrusion measuring out the end of a day's freedom, while the magic whisper of the mountain receded behind me. Did sensations such as those constitute the fugitive essence that people over the centuries had hymned in song and story, music and poetry and art, legend and belief, as the goal of living? And not for a moment's sensation only, but for a lifetime? Was it really the supreme goal called happiness? How did one know that a 'truer' completeness was not to be found beyond the next ridge, in the next experience? Was happiness not specific at all – but a still point in place and time where the co-ordinates of longing and effort met, where all striving could be halted, its supreme aim achieved?

That radio programme taught me that many people are not as curious about life as I had imagined, perhaps because, as with Hoffman and his reflection in the mirror, the boundary between the poetic imagination and the firm earth can be crossed without knowing it. And what seems to be fulfilment will usually not bear much examination. So Ecclesiastes was right after all.

Like Peer Gynt looking for the heart of life – in that superlative image of peeling the layers of the onion one by one – I had not found the heart either, nor would I have recognised it if I had. Long ago in Oxford, for a time I thought I did know – happiness was volition, freedom to do what you wanted. Then I saw that freedom alone was not the answer either, for there were so many people in that privileged world who had volition but were unhappy; you had to know what you wanted before you could use that freedom to obtain it.

It seemed that that bright, innocent youth in the Gorbals was talking to me in a way I had never heard before – who had intuited so much, who set out from the grimly essential Gorbals on a quest he was certain he could complete; and yet not certain at all, half-afraid that the goal did not exist. That might account for the many avatars I was destined to inhabit, knowing in advance that none would fit.

The years had been full of experiment in relationships, donning different versions of myself, avatars chosen to test where I had reached in the journey – days not always of wine and roses, or not for long enough. Werner had called them masks to hide behind while I experimented with the quest. With Werner, a refugee scientist met in Oxford, I had found a lasting affinity. There were many sirens, many avatars – a new one to fit each siren – a need as compelling as Hoffman's was to know that his reflection in the mirror was the true one.

As each flame subsided, usually inexplicably, I shifted to a different reflection. I was navigating in a world in which I was certain of one thing only: that I was never where I wanted to be. The answer – or *an* answer – which did not fit any of these suppositions, came unexpectedly.

THREE

Mr Wolf and the Messiah

CERTAINLY IT SHIFTED MY VIEW OF LIFE, AND MY COURSE, more crucially than I realised at the time.

In the early 1960s I had committed myself to work in the Third World, convinced that I must put to the test feelings of compassion, and a vision of taking part in the historic quittance owed by the West. Later I would be chastened to realise how little I knew of yet another view of the human predicament. At the same time, by a divinely mischievous turn of fate, a new avatar was about to seize me – this time not a fleeting one.

One evening, by chance choosing a path never trodden before, the Gorbals must have nodded and relaxed its grip on the reins.

At a party where I knew few people, I was drawn to Jacqueline, unknown to me, beautiful, sensitive, poetic dreamer, in a black satin dress with a ruff of the same material rising to bouffant silky dark hair. She glowed as if the sun shone within. We talked as if there was no past we had not already shared; of poetry, of dreams translating visions into reality. The other guests moved round us and mixed and turned and mixed again; and we remained rooted where we had met, at a window overlooking London's Marylebone High Street – then still possessed of a private, domestic ambience, of romantic mystery that might have been congenial to Wilkie Collins – a few hundred paces from where we would one day set up house and have children.

But I was not yet sure. After that evening, though impatient to see her again, I wanted to know if destiny really meant what it appeared to be offering. I challenged it to prove itself. Would she telephone as promised? If she did, I was right, and it was important. She did phone. My world would change in a way not foreseen, but I knew it was the road I had needed to find.

I saw the old quest for what it had become – fleeing from shadows and from the Gorbals. Now it had come into its own again, the original courage regained for a fresh set of encounters with life. I had recovered the unfathomable certainty of the Mitchell Library days: 'Recherche épuisante de moi . . .'

At the time I did not see the link between Jacqueline entering my life and these perspectives changing, but it was there. I felt free to follow visions from long ago, though in forms not at once recognisable. Soon I was winging across the world on international work, but the greatest distances were within.

I sometimes met Bill and Bernard in Rome. Bill, my principal Oxford friend, was now in international finance; Bernard, no longer a revolutionary, moved in the ill-defined world between the trade unions and politics. Rome was a convenient crossing point in our respective travels, and we spent long evenings in talk in Alfredo alla Scrofa or the Café Greco. On the surface, from their separate points of view, they were there to understand the Italian Miracle and, later, the political shifts in Italy dubbed the 'historic compromise'.

Essentially, however, we weighed in the balance our interior journeys and compromises, a theme that would soon surface in zeitgeist parlance as the 'mid-life crisis'. But we recoiled from putting it so bluntly, for that would be to concede that compromise with life was now part of the given. But it was in the air between us.

I thought of compromise in Father's life, and that of poor Mr

Wolf who had lived on optimism all the way downhill; and Bernard's father and the rest: not compromise but a continual retreat; not reassessment but capitulation.

I remembered a crisp spring day, walking with Father along the Broomielaw, the long quay on the north bank of the Clyde opposite the Gorbals, where small cargo boats moored. Over it hung a cloud of smells, of sawdust and straw and horse dung, and aromatic vapours from bales and packing cases, fascinating for a boy of about ten, evoking dreams of romantic adventure in distant places. I had learnt that Father took me on this walk when he was especially troubled, when I must have sensed his heightened unhappiness, but I loved him intensely at those times, with the sense of his strength beside me like a great tree, closer than at any other time. His discontent with himself must have hit me harder than I knew. I wished I could wave a wand and rescue him and make his life peaceful, and that we could always be as close as at those moments. We paced along in silence for a while before he spoke: 'I have something to tell you – something I have decided to do. I am going to live with a woman – I mean, *we* are.'

The words 'live with a woman' had no special significance for me, only that we would have another person in the house. That puzzled me, for we had only one bed, which I shared with him – the 'concealed bed' it was called – behind a curtain on a string in the kitchen alcove beside the coal range, where I slept against the wall so that he could get into bed without climbing over me and waking me when he came in late from the gambling club. He usually did wake me, though he was careful not to light the gas or a candle and undressed quietly in the dark – or as often as not in the grey light of dawn coming through the grimy window panes. Since in the obscurity it was hard to tell from his expression if he had lost and was in a bad mood, I pretended to be asleep.

This was one of the periods when he had grown a moustache, which spread, clipped and bristly, along the whole of his upper lip.

He occasionally smoothed it to the sides with forefinger and thumb opening out, especially when he was out of sorts or worried. He did so now, and said: 'We will live in her house in Abbotsford Place and you will have a bed of your own. It is time you slept on your own.'

Abbotsford Place was close by, a rung or so up the Gorbals ladder, where the closes and stairs were generally a little cleaner. Why would it be better for me there?

I wondered about the words: 'It is time.' Many Gorbals children shared a bed with their parents. Till that moment I had seen no significance in where I slept. Something unusual in his words or tone must have prompted me to speak more openly than I had ever dared before: 'Father, why are you saying this?' I had no idea that my words had a deeper meaning for him, and perhaps for me. I was astonished by his reply, especially by the emotion in his voice.

'I am not doing this because I need a woman — but it may be different for her . . .' He checked himself and smoothed his moustache again. He hurried on: 'There ought to be a woman to look after you. I know I can't do as much for you as you need – that is hard for a man. You will understand when you grow up.'

It crossed my mind that I had never heard the expression 'need a woman' before. I assumed that it had something to do with preparing food or cleaning the flat.

We walked in silence. I knew he had something else to say and began to feel frightened again.

'There are things God does not allow,' he said. 'A man is forbidden to sleep with a woman he is not married to. A woman must not sleep with a man she is not married to. But this is different. It is written that to preserve life comes before everything else, and I am doing this not because I want to but because *you* need better looking after. Your mother has been dead four years. I waited before doing this because of her. Because of what she meant to me, and means to me now. It is hard for me to do this, but I am doing it for the best.'

He talked on, but all I understood was that he was upset. The reason was beyond me. In his heavy-shouldered gait he strode force-fully along, staring straight ahead, jaw taut. I quickened my step to keep up with him. I wondered again why 'sleeping with' needed to be mentioned. God must know that people in the Gorbals shared beds? 'Sleeping with' must have a mysterious meaning. I asked: 'What *is* being married?'

He stopped and looked down at me, shaking his head, and walked on, his broad hard hand gripping mine tightly, pulling me along. He said: 'You ask hard questions but it is good. Being married is something God wants. No! Being married means . . .' He checked himself and smoothed his moustache.

I felt cold. I had crossed a frontier into a world where awesome things threatened on every side, where even Father, strong as he was, could not give me the guidance I wanted.

He said: 'It is hard for me to explain now. It is too early. I will explain it when you are older. There are rules in life you have to obey – God's rules – and never ask why. God never answers you. You have to trust Him. There is no other way.'

That moment, I realised many years later, was my first encounter with the idea of faith; though the word itself was unknown, I knew in some secret way that it must be something like the magic that focused so much of my life; one believed in it because one had to. It was part of the given. Like my magical visions, it must be a per-vasive, necessary power from whose enigmatic rules there was no escape. That was what Father seemed to be saying. Magic and faith, I would see in retrospect, were not very different.

My fears must have been sharpened by the prospect of leaving our own home and going to live under the roof of the unknown woman. Fear of her turned to antipathy when Father said I must call her Auntie – Auntie Hetty. That would be an affront to Aunt Rachel, my true aunt, Mother's sister, in whose one-room dwelling at the back of Uncle Zalman's clothes repair shop in Main Street there was always warmth, a precious sense of belonging that I wished I could take home with me, but the visits had to be concealed from Father, for he had forbidden me to go there. He considered that Aunt and Uncle had betrayed him by helping my sisters when they left home about a year before. I was puzzled that he saw that kindness as betrayal.

It would be another ten years before I began to understand the Hetty experiment. Father saw many things with devastating clarity, but his bitterness, his failing hope, could distort his vision. Here was a childless woman living alone; here was a child without a mother; the two should combine naturally and relieve him of a burden as well as a sense of inadequacy towards me. Could he really have expected nature alone to do all that? In his strong heart many storms raged. Even at his most reasonable, he seemed to expect things to work because he desperately wanted them to.

I must have intuited – as a child does, struggling to make sense of unfamiliar things – that I was a burden he longed to unload, so that he could challenge life properly, a wish that must have begun to stir in *me*, an unthinking impatience to be my own self. Looking back, it was impossible to imagine what it was like to be in his shoes. Still, as I had no existence apart from him, I had to be part of whatever answer he found. I must have had some idea that I stood in the way, and felt guilt at the thought. It was not my fault, and yet it was.

I must have sensed his uncertainty about this move. A numbness of the spirit must have seized him, for how otherwise could he have expected that other woman to take my mother's place and set him free?

How could I question him – even if I dared – when I was not sure what it was that troubled him? Mine were cloudy perceptions, which must have increased my feeling that nothing in life would ever be comprehensible, that I would always be trying to recapture meanings that had raced past me.

About a week later, my heart full of foreboding, a brown paper bag under my arm – he had a bigger one – we walked the hundred yards to her house: two rooms and kitchen that smelled of carbolic soap and furniture polish. She looked younger than my remembered image of Mother, not a reliable comparison because Mother had been dying. What Father had told me about the woman meant little. She was a widow. She ran a small business from home, a clothing club, a 'menodge' in the Gorbals vernacular, supplying goods on a weekly repayment system. Thin, with a ramrod back, she had a sharp, impatient voice, features lit by autumn redness, and moved with restless energy. I regarded her warily and must have shown it. Something about her, a sniff, a quick shift of attention, told me not to expect warmth.

She pointed to a tiny slit of a room containing a chair-bed and an upright wooden chair, and said in a distant voice that tried, unwillingly, to be kind, that I was to sleep there. New-looking linoleum covered the floor, patterned in small blue and white squares and springy under foot. I put my school books and exercise jotters on the wooden chair, with a brown paper bag containing vest and pants and socks that Father had washed, and stood wondering when I would see the familiar things of home again. The small window panes had no grime on them, and that was disturbing. I waited for Father to tell me what to do, how to get my bearings in this new, unfriendly world. He said nothing.

The three of us stood in silence, the walls of the narrow room pressing inwards, as though waiting for some part of the world to give way, but nothing did. The whole of creation weighed me down. She told me that she and Father would sleep in the larger room, and I must not enter it. I looked up at Father, expecting him to contradict her. How could I be forbidden to go into the room where he slept? He was silent, and smoothed his moustache.

I reminded myself that Father had kept on our own house; perhaps there was hope after all.

The experiment lasted about a month. She did not take to me, and made no effort to conceal it. I was too young to know that she would have seen *any* youngster as an inconvenience.

I cannot claim that I deliberately wrecked the experiment. However, a game I invented must have destroyed what promise it may have had. Father, perhaps to sweeten the move for me, had given me a shiny new penknife. In an idle moment, alone in the little room, I tossed the knife in the air, blade open and pointing upwards, fascinated to watch the blade turn and point downwards, to embed itself in the bouncy blue linoleum. I tried to aim the upward throw so that the blade would land in a particular square, not easy to do; soon there was a large patch of little slits where the point had hit. One afternoon when I came in from school – Father was out at work – she asked me, in unfamiliar, breathless, sugary tones, to lend her my knife for a minute. Trustingly I handed it over. She tucked it away in the pocket of her black apron and spat out, bent almost double in fury: 'Ye'll never see i' again – never! Look wha' ye've done tae ma new lino! There's a devil in ye, that's what!'

I went and stood with my forehead against the window, hating her for deceiving me to get the knife. She went to the kitchen, and after a few minutes shouted: 'Ye might as well come an' eat yer tea anyway – tha'll make nae difference!' I did not answer and she did not shout again. I heard her pace about the kitchen, grumbling to herself.

When Father came in from work the place was full of frozen silence. He had said nothing about the holes in the linoleum; but I guessed that something about it had passed between them that morning, and now he would take some action that he had brooded on during the day. I was going to get a hiding – I bit my lip in preparation. His mouth held tight, he was the image of suppressed anger. He made a sideways move of his hand to tell me to keep out of the way. She stood in the kitchen doorway, arms folded, a look of challenge in her red face. With a gesture of the chin he motioned her into their bedroom, followed her and closed the door. I heard his low, firm mutterings that seemed to remonstrate with her, and her strident complaint and then entreaty – a stiff-necked reckoning. It did not last long, perhaps ten minutes. The door opened and he came out alone. I saw her standing facing the window, her back turned. He carried a large brown paper bag under his arm, which I guessed, with a lift of the heart, contained the few belongings he had brought with him. 'Get your things,' he said.

I snatched them up and ran out of the front door ahead of him and down the curved flight of stone stairs to the close below and the street, and then all the way to our own close and waited there, then followed him up the stairs to our home.

As we went in he made his only reference to the experiment, his usual fatalistic underlining of sad events: '*Es shtayt geschrieben!*' It is written! It is God's will.

I knew it would hurt him to show my joy at this release. Other, deeper emotions would surface as the years passed: compassion for his forlorn battle with circumstance, the fading of time and strength, faulty assessments of people and the world.

A friend of his had lived in our house during our absence, Mr Wolf, a machinist in a garment factory. When we came in he was sitting by the fire in shirt sleeves and braces reading *Die Zeit*, a Yiddish newspaper printed in large format in Hebrew characters. He glanced up and read Father's face in an instant and without a word got to his feet and put a kettle on the fire to make tea. When they had drunk glasses of milkless tea through lumps of sugar, Father went out and bought food – bread, eggs, potatoes, herrings. He did not speak of our time away, but both men busied themselves in silence making a meal for the three of us, occasionally stealing a glance at each other and at me. Then we sat down and ate, mostly in silence.

Afterwards, they sat by the grate and lit cigarettes and brooded and talked and brooded again, the silences longer. The meanings were clothed in an impenetrable magic, and I wished I could read the feelings in the depths beneath; what I heard was not reason but poetic incantation that each recognised and affirmed with a nod or shrug, arcane conjuring of fate. Then Father put some more coal on the fire, and they sat in a much longer silence. Weary now from the miracle of release and the effort of trying to penetrate this secret language of theirs, I crawled into the concealed bed and slept.

Mr Wolf had brought a double mattress with him, spread on the bare floor of the bedroom; all his other belongings were in two battered brown suitcases that lay against a wall with their lids open, for there was not even a table or chair in the room to rest anything on. I tried to imagine what landslides of life had brought him here, isolated, pieces of his existence having fallen away with each previous move from refuge to refuge. There was a cupboard in the room with shelves, but so accustomed must he have been to the impermanence of any stopping place that he had not bothered to use it. At last he followed Father's urging and emptied the suitcases into the cupboard, a few shirts and collars, woollen vests and long pants and stockings thin from much washing, books, letters in strange jagged handwriting, bundles of closely written papers; most interesting of all, several large sepia portrait photographs in silver frames. The subjects, posed beside traditional studio props, carved lecterns, chairs with buttoned upholstery, rustic gates, had an air of importance, dressed in a way I had never seen before, men in high-buttoned jackets, cravats gathered below wing collars in what must have been silver rings, women in long tight-waisted dresses buttoned to the chin, wide sleeves tapering to the wrist – voices from another world.

Always neatly turned out in grey suit and trilby hat, Mr Wolf was slight, birdlike in movement, with long narrow face, shiny bald head with tufts of grey hair above the ears. His speech crackled excitedly, especially when he repeated a favourite mantra: 'I know what the world has got to do.' He did not go to the gambling club, but spent much time in the Gorbals library reading newspapers, or at the Workers' Circle rooms in Oxford Street arguing about the fashioning of the socialist world he was sure was on its way.

His fingers were stained hazelnut brown by cigarettes smoked down to the last shred of tobacco. Paroxysms of coughing, when his narrow chest rumbled with phlegm, left him gasping – and Father, who did not smoke so continuously, became anxious, threw his own cigarette away, and pleaded with him: 'It breaks my heart to hear you – wait another hour before you light the next one.'

Mr Wolf, when he got his breath back, shook his head: 'What is done is done – it's too late to change.'

Father told me that there were many isolated men like Mr Wolf in the Gorbals, left high and dry by the waves of migration that had swept through from Eastern Europe and on to America, this country being for many of them only a stopping place. The full poignancy of their state came to me only many years later. Some, through caution or because money was too short, had left wives and family behind, intending to save what was needed to send for them. Sometimes, through ill-luck or improvidence, they failed to save enough money, and were marooned in the Gorbals while their families pined for them and for release far away in the ironically named *der Heim*, the homeland that did not want them. For many, that separation was final. Others, cheated by officials on their way – a normal experience – had devoted what money they had left to send their families on ahead of them to the Golden Land, intending to follow as soon as they had saved enough for their own tickets. Some succeeded and continued the journey. Some were rescued by relatives who had gone on ahead and prospered, and sent money for them to join them. A defeated rearguard was left behind in the Gorbals.

Of that remainder some proclaimed that the socialist Messiah would come sooner in this country than in America, and it was wise to remain here to await that day. Mr Wolf was one of them. Father saw through the pathetic excuse, and I must have sensed the sadness and scepticism in his voice as he told me of it – not to be understood till many years later. 'Let them have their dreams and their excuses,' he said. 'What else have they got?' Father could be implacably stoical, as Alec was. He preferred to outface destiny, lest he deceive himself with false comfort.

Father and Mr Wolf cooked traditional dishes of home: grated potatoes baked in the oven, eaten with pickled herrings; occasionally chicken soup made from a quarter of a carcase – many Gorbals folk blessed their luck if they could afford even that minimal amount – with *lockshen* (pasta), or *knaydlach* (dumplings) sometimes filled with onions baked dark brown. In the tiny kitchen, stuffy and warm, with curtains of coal smoke hanging over our heads, those meals were wonders of luxury and reassurance, rich with whispers of faith and hope from a distant past. In the steam rising from my plate I conjured people I had never seen, who told me that I was fully part of them, and I imagined strands of my emerging identity stretching back to them, held like reins in their distant hands.

Afterwards, cigarettes between their lips, Father and Mr Wolf talked of the world, of life, while they washed dishes and utensils and dried them. Then they set two wooden chairs side by side facing the fire and sat in silence, leaning forward with elbows on knees, looking into the flames. I imagined them drawing up to the surface a secret world they wished they could rejoin. Then they talked, often into the small hours, in long soliloquies or in breathless exchanges, seeming to draw strength from each other.

Sometimes Father hurried out to the gambling club. Mr Wolf shifted his chair so as to sit directly under the pale yellow gas mantle that hung from a thin pipe in the wall above the high mantelpiece, put on wire-framed spectacles and read a library book, while I tried to understand a timeless significance in his fragile figure. Sometimes, catching sight of me staring at him, he closed the book and spoke of socialism – a Messianic salvation – as if I understood every word, his thin face shining with excitement. With a child's acute sympathy I knew he was a good person and was drawn to him.

When they both stayed in I was happy. I undressed quietly so as not to distract them, and climbed into the concealed bed behind the curtain and listened, not to the words but to the harmonics beneath. Their sadness coursed through me. I wished I was old enough to know what it meant for them, and feel it as they did.

I learned that Mr Wolf was a *landsmann* of Father's – from the same part of the world. I was thrilled to sense the important link this created, as if a lamp of the spirit burst into bright flame, in ways of speaking, of referring to events and people – even to the harsh vicissitudes of life they both knew. As they talked into the night, and the noises from the tenement and the street faded, the world became charged with new magic in the linked resonances of their voices. It seemed that they traced old dreams, recalled small victories and looked for lessons in them, paused from time to time to peer timidly into the future, now cruelly foreshortening. They recalled their youth as a time of supreme certainty they wished they could summon again if only for a day. In another vision I imagined them as lost mariners trying to extract guidance from an old chart whose inscriptions were in a language once familiar, now unknowable. I willed myself to believe in their dreams and make them mine, and make them come true.

I wondered why Mr Wolf and Father, old and strong and wise, clung to visions in which they themselves seemed to have lost faith. Sometimes, for no reason, hope stirred in them, and they went about for a day as if reborn; and I knew that Father hated those times, which he knew would be punished by the return of dispirited gloom. Was there *never* a clear way to be found? Were dreams always the wrong ones? If only I could discover what the right paths were and show them the way, so that they would not go on taking the wrong course, nursing the wrong hopes. But who could I ask, where could I go, to learn that? I never heard Father or Mr Wolf speak of such a wish. Once youth was gone, it was part of the given to suffer.

For them, as for me at that age, success was fulfilment of *any* kind, an expression of identity. That there was only one right identity for each person, and the true quest was to find it and follow it faithfully, took hold of me much later, in the Oxford days. But the quest itself must have been forming as I lay in the concealed bed and listened to their meditative voices probing the night.

In later years, thinking of Mr Wolf, I remembered that although he talked of reason as the only true beacon through life, in the ordinary run of speech he constantly invoked God and Moses – *Moshe robbaynoo*, Moses our teacher – as Father also did, imprint of the tradition they shared. I must have seen that they were not really cut off from the old faith, as in their defeated state they sometimes pretended. They felt its magnetism still, more than half in fear of it.

Mr Wolf's tilting at 'what to do with life' puzzled me, because it suggested that life was a distinct entity, complete in itself, waiting for one to decide what to 'do' with or leave alone – as if one really had that choice. How *could* one leave it alone? Could life steer by itself? It was a terrifying question. Lying in the concealed bed listening to their talk I tried to visualise life 'managing' by itself, and a recurrent nightmare returned: of countless massive, dark objects hurtling through the sky and threatening to collide but somehow escaping – only just! And no one would tell me why they were there, and why I myself was among them. I sensed that when Mr Wolf and Father talked of leaving life alone they were really saying: 'We have tried to discover what life wanted of us and failed – now let life tell us what it wants us to do.'

Neither of them believed that it would. They pretended to sit back with folded hands and wait for life to speak; a vision that haunted me ever afterwards, for it meant that there was no hope whatever. If life had not 'spoken' to them in all the years, why should it do so now? To my ten-year-old mind, life was like the sky and the stars whose transcendent magic must be matched with magic of one's own. That was the terrible challenge that they had never accepted.

I spent many nights inventing images for their plight. One of them returns even now. They were trying to make their way through a maze in which a demon had placed an impassable obstacle. Mr Wolf insisted that there was a clear way through, but the struggle to find it was the 'price life makes us pay for living'. But you must be willing to pay the price – and that meant you had to believe there *was* a way through! A circular solution.

So belief was a kind of magic? Years later I saw that by 'belief' Mr Wolf meant faith, and the riddle – how to navigate by faith and reason at one and the same time – defeated him.

Father cut through it by saying simply: 'God holds you tight in His harness no matter how far you try to stray!'

Mr Wolf must have suspected that reason was not the support he pretended. As for Father, I must have intuited at the time that he was spiritually exhausted and knew it, and all that was left was a directionless hope that capriciously stirred in him, bringing painful reminders of times when he had answered its call and found he had given the wrong answer. He may even have wished that he could copy Mr Wolf's rationalism, but he had closed that door long before. He once said to him: 'The trouble with you is – you think with your *heart* and call it reason!' He was in some things too clear-headed for his own peace of mind.

I was never sure how much comfort those talks brought them. I sometimes wondered if they were a necessary ritual to help them believe that hope was still possible – that by some remote chance a way of redemption would suddenly open. But when each session ended, and the real world rushed in again, I saw bitterness almost palpably return – dreamers in an enchanted cavern awakening to find that nothing had changed. Long afterwards I saw that they persisted for another reason: they did not know how much time they had left.

A few months later an answer came. Mr Wolf had sometimes ended an attack of coughing by bringing up blood, and one evening there had been more blood than usual, which he pitifully tried to catch in his hand to stop it staining his white shirt. Then he groaned and slid sideways, and Father reached out in time to stop him falling to the floor. He moved him, still sitting in the chair, nearer the bed, drawing the curtain aside so that he could rest on the blanket half-lying, half-sitting. Then he rushed to the door, pulling his braces over his shoulders, telling me to make sure Mr Wolf did not go too near the fire. At the pub on the corner, the landlord telephoned for an ambulance.

Father had warned me never to try to lift Mr Wolf if he was ill. I waited beside his chair, wishing I knew what to do, knowing — and yet trying not to — that something terrible was happening. He must have been in a kind of faint, for when I said, fearfully: 'Mr Wolf, can I do anything?' his eyes flickered open, and he may have been trying to speak but he only groaned, and moved in a kind of rhythmic shiver, blood oozing from his mouth. I stroked his head as tears flowed down my face. I hoped I helped him a little, as I had been unable to help Mother in what turned out to have been her last days. The ambulance came and I followed the men as they manoeuvred the stretcher down the tight curve of the steep stone stairs, slippery with dirt, and through the narrow close to where the ambulance waited, with a group of curious onlookers clustered round. Father told me to go back upstairs. There was nothing for me to do but wait; Mr Wolf would be well looked after in hospital. He went with the ambulance to the Royal Infirmary and I went upstairs to our flat and waited and sat in Mr Wolf's chair that was still warm, and stared at the blobs of deep red blood on the bed cover, knowing but pushing the knowledge away.

I did not see Mr Wolf again. Father, when he came back from the hospital, had told me Mr Wolf was very ill, but not that he was dying. Later I was angry because he had given me false hope. I did not know that 'very ill' was what people said when someone was dying. I wept for days. Why was God so cruel?

In the years after I left the Gorbals I saw more deeply into their talks, and why they had clung to their illusions. Time had sped on and abandoned them, leaving only the stubborn hope that a miracle *was* possible, that redemption could still come. No wonder Father had sometimes interrupted their talk and gone to the gambling club – where miracles *did* sometimes happen.

I knew I had learned something from Mr Wolf too momentous to grasp all at once – which Father in his own stoic fashion had also hinted at – that to dream of imposing your own ideal visions on life was a mistake that could bring terrible retribution. Life had no patience with dreams of perfection – or with dreams at all. Or perhaps *their* dreams had always been the wrong ones? But how could dreams *always* be wrong? God must know why. Father had once said, on one of those Broomielaw walks: 'If God had intended life to fit our dreams He would have made it so!'

Those words resonated in my mind like a spell, and returned to question me again and again in places I had never expected to visit, prompted by events I never thought to experience.

Looking back in later years I saw that in their translation across Europe to the Gorbals – as in mine from the Gorbals to Oxford and after – Father and Mr Wolf had carried the unredeemed past with them, which they too could neither absorb into their new life nor discard. In those long hours of listening to them from behind the curtain in the kitchen, I became infected with their distrust of past and future. They were gods. They knew infinitely more than I did, more than I ever would. Unawares I took over their accrued pain and made it mine.

When they spoke of the Messiah coming, they could have been speaking of a friend confidently awaited, his journey merely delayed. He might appear the very next moment and one must be ready to receive Him. I must have asked myself if in their secret hearts they knew that for them it would never happen. A child rejects doubt as too terrible to countenance – it must be certainty or nothing; and so, sensing that their belief mocked them and their doubt hurt them, I tried in magic to endow them with my own desperate certainty on their behalf.

That counterfeit certainty must have mysteriously prepared me – in ways not understood even now – for the near-catastrophe at the Snaid Falls, and that cry of 'I don't care!'. But, before that, another trauma intervened, where magic was of no help either.

When my fourteenth birthday was near, Father said I must tell the school I would be leaving that term – there was no hope of his being able to afford to keep me at school beyond the obligatory age. I would have to go out to work. I wondered why he did not tell them himself. He was big and strong and could surely take that burden from me, knowing as he must have done how I hungered to stay on at school. Then I remembered that he shrank from confronting officialdom of any kind, as many immigrants did, and forgave him.

I had dreamed of staying on at school and then by a miracle going on to university, dreamed and prayed even though Father had often warned me – a strange anger entering his voice which must have been guilt – that there was no possibility of it, and so staying on at school would be a waste of money even if he *could* afford it.

I saw boys in the streets who obviously *were* set on that course, from Hutcheson's Grammar School, the school on the eastern edge of the Gorbals, recognisable in long dark trousers and neat dark jacket, white shirt and tie, the 'Hutchie' badge in their buttonhole; and I cursed them under my breath, knowing I should not, for they were not to blame for being on a road denied to me. Later on I would see their seniors, university students, in the Mitchell Library on days when I was laid off from the factory. How carefree they were, those golden young men. Their confidence dimmed my sight and I hated them too – and I told myself again that it was not their fault; which made my hatred turn sour, for I knew where the fault lay: with Father. And that thought also brought guilt.

Years later, trying to reason the 'fault' away from him, no sophism would do – the bitter verdict of the child was implacable. I wondered whether Father had known it at the time. I imagine he did.

Of course I had no thought of any worldly benefit from going to university. I only knew that I wanted to go on learning for the thrill of it.

And so, on a doom-laden Monday morning, I trod a stone corridor, its walls coated with large white tiles, poorly lit, a damp, funereal place. At the end of it was a dark-panelled door, the head-master's room. Was there still a chance? Would he say a magic word to change the world for me? I tried not to believe in the finality of what Father had told me to say; but I did not believe in my attempt to conjure magic. The world moved in its ordained way, and Father's words had to be spoken.

The headmaster was someone I had seen only from afar, a dignified figure in clerical grey suit and white shirt and grey tie. He was seated at a desk piled with papers and thin files. The walls were lined with tall bookshelves filled with books, and that sight brought envy so overwhelming that I wanted to turn and run away. How wonderful it would be to have all that knowledge belonging to me alone.

'Well, laddie,' he said, getting up and stepping round the desk towards me. 'I see you're admiring my books? It's good to value learning!' He stopped abruptly. He must have been told of my purpose, and was now struck by the pain and fear in my face.

I had first of all told my class mistress what Father wanted me to say, hoping she would convey it for me. She was a brisk woman probably in her forties, with fair hair in a bun, just beginning to show streaks of grey. As one of her 'good' pupils, I had an easy time with her, but she could be severe with some of the other boys in the class of forty-four. She turned away for a moment and took her glasses off and wiped her eyes, then faced me again and said: 'Don't you worry – you'll be all right.' And then, features suddenly very serious, she went on: 'If you must leave, you must, but I'll miss you – we all will. You are a good scholar. You're top of the class, after all, which makes it doubly sad. Still, you will make your way in the world, I am sure of it.'

I wanted to ask her *how* that could happen, but the words refused to form themselves. I only thought: 'If they are so sure of how good I am, why can't they do something to help me stay?'

Then she said: 'The headmaster must hear it from you yourself. That is important.'

I took this as betrayal, insisting that I must face the headmaster. In retrospect there was another reason. In those hard times of financial stringency – depression, days of 'economy' – everyone had to protect themselves, and not show their feelings too openly, which might be interpreted as criticising higher authority. To suggest special arrangements for individuals, if possible at all, was not to be done lightly.

The headmaster continued, his voice compressed, formal, watchful: 'What have you come to say to me?'

I blurted out: 'Father hasn't got the money, sir. He's told me to say I can't stay at school.'

'I know,' he said, and looked down at the floor, hands thrust into jacket pockets. 'I am sorry. You are one of our best pupils. You ought to be aiming for university. We haven't many like you. And so . . .' He seemed lost for words.

I misunderstood his silence. I thought he was passing judgment on Father and waited for me to defend him – but how could I? I was torn between duty and desire – and saw that my desire was without power of any kind. The stuffing had been knocked out of me.

He spoke again: 'What is your father's work? And what does your mother say about this?'

'Mother's dead, sir – when I was six. And Father's unemployed.'

The word 'unemployed' seemed to stir him to sudden alertness. It did not occur to me till years later that his reaction was a response to current battles in the streets – in those days of Wal Hannington and the National Unemployed Workers' Movement, whose street

56

propaganda had endowed the word with powerful magic in Red Clydeside.

He straightened himself and frowned, as if he wanted to back away. With a testy click of the tongue he said: 'No, no, laddie – not *un*-employed – you mean *dis*-employed. Call things by their proper names.'

I nearly let the tears go in a flood. Did it matter whether it was 'un' or 'dis'?

I heard the footsteps of another boy approaching along the echoing corridor behind me, perhaps on the same errand. The headmaster's attention shifted for a moment, then he added: 'The way things are, with the streets full of the disemployed, things will be hard, but I will write you a good reference – you deserve it – for you to show to employers.'

I wondered what use that would be, for Father was talking about taking me to be apprenticed to a barber, as a barber's soap boy. Even at this last moment, hope flickered; the headmaster might utter some piece of magic to save me. None came.

'Goodbye and Godspeed,' the headmaster said, heaved a sigh and went back round the desk and sat down to greet the next boy.

Walking back between the cold tiled walls, the idea of fighting this stroke of destiny did not occur to me. That the demons within might be brewing up something for the future did not strike me either – who could fight this enigmatic world? One thought alone tugged at the heart: those packed bookshelves, by their mute presence, were the most telling statement of my deprivation. How could I fight that world? In that stone corridor, no answer came.

FOUR

Poisoned Chalice

NOT LONG AFTER I MARRIED JACQUELINE A NEW AVATAR brought changes in myself as profound as those that followed my transition to Oxford – in identity, in world view. Whether the marriage and these changes were linked is a nice question, impossible to determine but forever intriguing. One tends to say, borrowing from folk wisdom, that you make a certain shift in life when you *know* you are ready. But were you ready long before? I prefer to think that I had been ready for some time – how long I have no idea – and then destiny presented the opportunity.

The new frame of mind took me into international work, mainly in the strangely named Third World, a label that had entered international usage at the 1955 Bandoeng Conference, to denote countries outside the two power blocs of communist and non-communist countries. It has lost that meaning, but since *that* Third World comprised in the main the poorer, less-'developed' countries, the label is no longer a political description but an economic and social one. Its peoples reached out for something called 'development' – a term borrowed from economics but with wider, increasingly indeterminate social and ethical meanings. At its most basic, development meant the attempt to copy the technology and ways of life of the industrially advanced countries of the West – in the received opinion of those days the only road to fulfilment. That view is slowly changing, in ways I helped to encourage.

Much of the received opinion believed – and still does – that these Western countries had a moral duty to assist that development. To fulfil it, a development industry has grown up to organise and fund, and to a considerable extent staff, 'development aid'.

I began to question the wisdom of encouraging 'backward' peoples to follow the example of the industrial West too closely, where traditional communities and their values had broken down under the Siren attractions of consumerism and technological change. I felt a certain guilt at first, remembering the Gorbals belief that purchasing alone was the key to happiness. Then I reminded myself that I had rejected that belief long ago in my Oxford essay, and still held the views expressed in it. What I now learned in the field convinced me that development aid could be a poisoned chalice presenting mankind with the most dangerous dilemma of the modern age.

In expressing these doubts, when addressing conferences or writing or in governmental discussions, I learned to be wary of being wrongly understood to be arguing that Third World peoples should be denied the 'benefits' of progress. Sometimes the suspicion was implied; often it was explicit: 'Why should the West have a monopoly on progress? As for the supposed social damage you talk about, if the West cannot solve their social problems that is *their* affair, not ours!'

There was no simple answer to that either. Development had become charged with powerful emotion; it was a latter-day Philosopher's Stone, to be pursued at any price. In the 1960s and 1970s especially, I campaigned, wrote and lobbied, aware that the indiscriminate lust for development expressed a historic shift of cultures, and of the received view of fulfilment itself. At a United Nations

conference on strategies of development, I presented a paper
entitled *Development vis-à-vis Human Fulfilment — some neglected socio-
economic questions* which was later included in evidence to the House
of Commons Select Committee on Overseas Development, and
published in its Report on 24 July 1973. I argued that the proper
preliminary question should be: what *kind* of progress? How did a
particular culture understand fulfilment? And then tailor progress
to fit. Few considered that to be necessary; after all, many Western
peoples had given up trying to answer it for themselves, so why
should they expect the Third World to do so? Some interests
perhaps opposed it because the development industry preferred to
continue unchanged. Others claimed that the West had little right
to ask such questions at all — it owed a historic moral debt to the
Third World because of past domination; the poisoned chalice thesis
was an excuse to avoid paying it.

Some forms of aid had created urgent problems. Unrealistic
commercial lending to some underdeveloped countries had trapped
them in crippling debt-service burdens. Since it became obvious
that it was impossible to treat such loans realistically, a common
'remedy' was to write them off, or, in a conventional euphemism,
reschedule them.

Political vested interest revealed itself in bizarre ways. At one
conference an exchange between a Latin American delegate and one
from a small African country showed the absurdity of some
influential thinking about progress. The Latin American expounded
the Marxist dogma of the class war as a necessary process. The
African, a cultivated man, listened in obvious wonder. At last he
said: 'Please tell me — what is this class war you speak of? If I
understand you correctly, we have no classes in my country.'

Back came the impatient answer: 'That is because you have been
kept in a backward state by the oppressors. You must hurry up and
create classes!' He was not joking; that was clear. The African looked
grave, and said he must think about it.

It was salutary to see the Third World from a necessary position of detachment, often hard to maintain. As a small example, in the Indian sub-continent it took me a little time to get used to hearing myself addressed or referred to as Glasser Sahib. I asked myself what Glasser Sahib could possibly have to do with the Gorbals – recalling that I had felt similar disbelief in the early Oxford days when for the first time I was styled 'Mr' or 'gentleman'. I had to remind myself that 'Sahib' was simply a courteous form of address, to be distinguished from the egregious significance it had acquired in agitprop usage.

In night flights over the Gulf, the sight of reddish-yellow plumes of burning oil in the blackness below, doubtless economically justified, evoked thoughts of mankind's propensity for wasting the world's riches, especially for ignoring the lessons of past improvidence such as the deserts behind the Mediterranean shores of Africa, once the granary of the Roman Empire.

On the ground my viewpoint was privileged, and I often felt guilty on that account; thus I could leave when I wished, but most denizens of the 'backward' country I was visiting could not.

Many old hands felt that little had changed except for the new people in authority, and the growth of a new wariness towards visitors and expatriate residents, especially if they were from the former colonial power. Sometimes, if they felt they could speak freely, they wondered whether the colonial rulers had been so bad after all. Had they perhaps relinquished power too easily, and were to blame for leaving the people in the lurch? In view of the political volatility of some regions, I had to be careful at such moments, coming as I did from a former colonial power. Did such statements signify genuine sentiment, or ingratiation with an ulterior motive?

There were many echoes of the past, comic as well as poignant, and it was tempting to imagine that some might have been contrived to beguile the visitor. In Rawalpindi I was booked into the principal hotel at the time, named, improbably, Flashman's Hotel. It was intriguing to imagine the original of Thomas Hughes's anti-hero finding his way to this garrison frontier town poised between myth and reality, with whispers of the greatness of other ages, here on the route of the conquerors, close beneath the crossroads of continents on the roof of the world. Here, surely, nothing was improbable, when in the early November evening the gentle sunshine of an English day in May suddenly gave way to a glacial sky that sent icy fingers between one's ribs, straight from the mighty peaks in the mountains beyond Murree.

Place-names were elegiac voices from the past, joining the British time with that of Alexander – Sikandarpur (Alexandertown) in the Punjab, the disputed sites of his epic victory of the Jhelum, the silent cities of nearby Taxila. Then there were towns bearing names plainly of British origin, Murree (Murray), Abbottabad, Lyallpur. What manner of man was he whose name lived on in Murree, the little hill station that might have been planned as a copy of an English village, with glistening green hedges shielding dark brick houses with hooded doorways, a half-hour drive up the tortuous road to the 7,500-foot contour? What of Abbott of nearby Abbottabad, Lyall of Lyallpur, and the rest who had left their mark? Why had the names not been changed after independence? Would they ever be? Such retained symbols must mean something to those who now ruled over a collection of old fiefdoms welded together by the colonial power, though not the original meaning; like that of the line of British regimental badges carved in stone on the rock walls of the approach to the Khyber Pass, kept immaculate as if created yesterday.

Flashman's Hotel was an assembly of suites in bungalow style, on a broad avenue called The Mall – referred to by locals as Mall Road. Its sets of rooms were starkly but practically equipped: commodious cement shower room and toilet, sitting-room and bedroom, a gecko darting across the ceiling dealing with insects, an efficient but noisy air-conditioner, a telephone, and a bell-push for summoning a 'bearer'.

A stone's throw across The Mall was the Rawalpindi Club – familiarly the Pindi Club – with a sandy compound where a solitary tree gave sparse shade in the hot weather, the object of fierce competition to park under it in the middle of the day. Even those who succeeded in parking there might bring out a can of iced water when about to drive away, to throw over the blistering hot steering wheel before touching it. Forgetfully one day, I left a gramophone record in its cardboard sleeve on the back seat of my car when I went into the club for lunch; when I returned, the heat in the car had turned it into a piece of corrugated plastic.

Kiplingesque echoes were to be heard not only in the Indian sub-continent but in Africa. I wondered, sometimes, whether a Kipling reference was a standard form of politeness to a newly arrived British visitor.

Power, pride in new-found volition and furious haste in expressing it, were dominant. Competing interests sought popular support for ever-faster technological change and movement towards a consumer-ist society, a quest full of ironies for mainly agrarian economies. Extreme population growth, a cumulative function of improved health services and water supplies begun in colonial times, meant that demand must always be hot on the heels of earning capacity – and disappointment brought extremism. Reminders from Western experience, that too rapid modernisation, with its accompaniment of townward drift and agrarian decay, inexorably destroyed community and its supportive values, were denounced by populist rhetoric as attempts to keep Third World peoples in subjection.

Another sad irony of development was that the word 'liberation' attached to any slogan purified it. Thus there was 'liberation development', 'liberation planning', even 'liberation theology'. The wildest nostrums became respectable when marketed under the label of 'liberation economics'. Where did human relationships, ethics, morals find their place? Where was fulfilment? These were inconvenient questions.

In an East African school in a fertile valley, I sat in an English class of Third Grade boys, most of them in their mid-teens. The boy next to me was a broad-shouldered lad of sixteen. The teacher conducted a sentence-completion lesson. One sentence read: 'He has not passed the examination, therefore he is a —' The missing word was 'failure'. Had the teachers learned *their* English in this fashion, and had it been passed down unchanged from some distant epoch of indifference? In the crudest sense 'failure' was correct, but to use it in this general sense was woefully wrong. In this lesson, however, there was no hint of shades of meaning. Failure was failure! The boys bent their heads to write the word in the vacant place in their exercise books.

As a visitor I had to be silent. The stipulated answers were already printed in the teacher's lesson book; the responsibility for this way of teaching lay at a higher level.

I asked the boy what he would do when he finished school; would he work on the family holding? 'No,' he said firmly, 'I will go to the big town and be a truck driver.' At the words 'truck driver' he held his broad hands before him in the action of moving a huge steering wheel; the grasp on technology sent a radiant smile over his face. He was not going to be a failure.

I asked him what would happen to his family and the land they worked if he went away to the town.

'I will be rich,' he answered. 'I will send home much money.'

The West courted some of the new Third World leaders with admission to world status, perhaps in recognition of their peoples' aspirations. A strong impression in those countries was of disillusionment; the cornucopia of progress had failed to shower its riches on them.

Ancient divisions surfaced – tribal, cultural, linguistic, economic; dragons' teeth of discontent sown long before. There were many influences working against cohesion.

An example in Pakistan occasioned acid Pindi Club gossip. Pakistan was less then twenty years old; it was only a few years before the secession of East Pakistan to become Bangladesh in 1971. At the time, Pakistan consisted of two regions, referred to as the East and West Wings, separated by fifteen hundred miles of Indian territory – East Pakistan where Bengali was spoken, and West Pakistan that spoke Urdu. At governmental meetings where representatives of both Wings were present, people from one or the other sometimes had to interrupt themselves while speaking in their own language in order to make their meaning plain in English, the only true common language, a handicap that injured sectoral pride. That this irritant, on top of problems of physical communications, economic and cultural divergence, contributed to the finally crucial stresses cannot be doubted.

In the Indian sub-continent, nostalgia for a lost sense of confidence that Kipling had expressed, if it existed below the surface, was never made explicit. In other countries it was hinted at, especially in the middle levels of society, where people discreetly lamented the disappearance of former landmarks of behaviour and response, the feeling of knowing where you stood. A businessman, Mr Youssuf – name changed – said: 'Here is a small but important example. As things are now, if I want to get a particular position for a son or nephew, someone close to me, I give money to a man who promises to speak for me to some powerful person who will do the needful, and maybe I must give even more money to go higher still. And maybe this higher person will do something, or maybe someone else gives him more money than I did – and so I get nothing, and have lost my money into the bargain. In the British time it was different. It was often hard to get to see the British officer, but when I did, he listened to me without expecting money, and when I had explained my case he said: "I don't care *who* you want this position for. It's my duty to see that the best man gets the job. If your man is the best he'll get it. If not, he won't. That's all I have to say." Of course I knew this, but it was a matter of my personal honour to try.

The British officer's words were hard but they called it "fair play". You knew where you stood.'

I was never sure whether Mr Youssuf, or others who chose a safe moment to speak of the dependable attributes of the old order, did so as a kind of ingratiation. But why should they? As an outsider – and my stay temporary – they must have known that I was in no position to steer any advantage their way. The past was the past. And yet – who could say? The contemporary world was still in flux. It had not yet settled down to a solid dispensation. The future might one day go *their* way. Mr Youssuf and the others made a shrewd point. The British official had had to watch *his* step too. Stability demanded that everyone obeyed a known, predictable code. Statements like theirs illuminated the diverse faces of power.

They also brought home the sad truth that material gains – in effect progress in its many guises – brought no lasting contentment. Many people in such countries felt caught in a mirage world between old certainties and a potentially dangerous future. As always you had to get on the right side of power – there was no other way.

Wherever I went I was reminded that for a majority of Third World people life was lived at extremes. Average life expectancy was short, as little as thirty-five years, and competition to live even that long was severe. A high birth-rate was a form of insurance for old age and the unexpected – and rulers who tried to defeat that method of providing for uncertainty brought trouble on themselves. Of course it was part of progress to think of plans to raise life expectancy – medically, by improved hygiene and housing and food supplies – but how was one to defeat the corollaries of over-demand and hunger?

In a busy Karachi street, the heat intense, a group of children played happily in a flooded gutter of thick brown stinking water. A government official who was with me said that there was no drainage here. The smell and colour of the water put me in mind of the Leh Nullah in Pindi, a wide stream that was also a sewer, crossed by a bridge on the Murree Road – the only route to my house from the Secretariat building. The Leh Nullah's stench was so powerful that it caught you long before you reached the bridge; and I often tried to keep the car windows shut for the time it took me to cover the approach to the bridge, the bridge itself and the stretch of road beyond it – a slow business, for it was a busy road whose traffic might include camels, families on foot carrying burdens (and even squatting on the road), and horse-drawn tongas especially risky to follow closely, for on their two wheels they could turn without warning within their own wheel base. But to hold my breath for that length of time was impossible. So the Leh Nullah made itself known to me each day, and its smell, its brown surface, and the people who lived on its banks, are eloquent in memory still. Whole families lived there in tents made of torn sheets of plastic or tarpaulin, presumably using the brown water for every purpose of daily life – and children jumped in for their games. I thought of the Gorbals in comparison, the state of the streets I played in as a child, and the primitive ways of living. The details differed in degree but in some essentials the conditions were comparable. How then could one argue against consumerism for the Third World? Somewhere between the substance of life on the banks of the Leh Nullah and the breakdown of values in the industrial West, a pragmatic compromise cried out to be found.

The culture of power was evident everywhere. It existed to maintain selected certainties in the interests of stability – though in *whose* interests was another matter. I was given an exquisite demonstration, appropriately enough in a former proconsular club. These places, according to old hands who had stayed on – and the testimony of physical survivals such as English sporting prints on the walls – were much as they had always been. General Wassou – name changed – an impressive man of quiet charm, greeted me from a long chair: 'Let me offer you a Scotch. They've got the real thing today. None of that up-country stuff.'

The white-uniformed servant, ramrod straight, tunic glistening with highly polished brass buttons, brought my drink and a refilled glass for the General. We sat contemplating the hills in the middle distance through the glass door giving on to the veranda and the broad steps down to the compound. Even here in the shade, close to the noisy air-conditioner, the hard sun outside seemed to batter the air.

The General, given to long silences, had the gift of spreading tranquillity. He murmured: 'How are things?'

I pushed aside the official matters on my mind, in any case not to be spoken of in the club, and chose a safe topic for my reply: 'Oh, not too bad, except that I've got a problem – my supplies.'

Gravely he asked: 'Tell me what it is. I might be able to help.'

'Nice of you to ask. But I shouldn't think you can. The fact is they haven't come up yet.'

Supplies meant liquor. Officially the district was 'dry', but by a flight of pragmatism there were exceptions, the club itself of course, and a number of foreigners permitted to import duty-free personal supplies under 'diplomatic privileges'; not only diplomatic staff proper, but foreign advisers, aid officials, specialists – a term of wide application – attached to certain construction projects and industrial enterprises. As to the full extent of such exceptions it was probably unwise to enquire. Delays in the arrival of supplies, or 'shortages' when they did, cropped up in expatriate conversation.

His brow puckered. 'That *is* serious. Look here – let me make a note of what you need and I'll have it drawn from headquarters stocks and sent round to your quarters.'

Seeing me about to protest, he said: 'Not at all! Glad to help. When your supplies do come up, let me know and someone will come round and collect the replacements. Perfectly all right.'

He turned and snapped his fingers; when the servant came smartly to attention before him he told him to bring a sheet of club writing paper. The servant was back in a moment with the sheet of stiff cream paper. The General unbuttoned the flap of the breast pocket under the medal ribbons, took out a gold pen and held it poised.

I decided to pull his leg gently: 'Are you quite sure?'

He raised his brows a fraction: 'Of course I'm sure! Come on, I'll jot down what you want.'

'But you're dry here! Apart from the club?'

He leaned back and a slow grin appeared: 'All right! It's not the first time I've heard that one.' He glanced round the near-empty room, leaned towards me and tapped himself on the chest: 'We're the *army*! Nuff said, eh? Now, then, let's have the list.'

'Nuff said' summed it up. Power was the answer – and always would be.

He must have thought further about that tap on his chest. After some minutes he sat up, glanced round the room again and leaned closer: 'If you want to be philosophical about things, our position is interesting – I mean the army. I remember, at Staff College, the lectures about Clausewitz – what he said about the use of a reserve force. It went like this: "The ideal position is that the Reserve must never be used." It makes sense, doesn't it? The Reserve must always be *there* – but *as* a reserve! Once you commit your Reserve, you no longer *have* one! Then things become tricky. So our job is to maintain power without using it! And that calls for *very* nifty footwork.'

The bottles, in a sealed wooden box, were delivered a couple of hours later. The following week I bought the General a Scotch in the club and told him my supplies had come up. The next day an orderly from headquarters collected the replacements and gave me a receipt.

Later that same day I attended a government reception. As usual at formal gatherings, only soft drinks were served. From across the gilt-encrusted room the General toasted me with his glass of Coca-Cola and winked.

The reception was for a World Bank team. The talk touched on growth rates and debt service, though in general terms only.

The question of the poisoned chalice was outside the team's terms of reference. Its members represented the Faustian compact that the West and the Third World had made: 'We will not ask what brings happiness. We will settle for progress no matter what the consequences.'

It could hardly be otherwise. For the West, 'development' was the supposedly neutral creed on which it had grown rich and powerful. Who would dare to deny that the gains had outweighed the losses? Yet how could you assess gains and losses when there was no common measure, no 'like with like' to compare? Well, there *was*, but only by subjective judgement *after* the event; and who would dare tell the people of the Leh Nullah, or the Gorbals, that the 'costs' of progress were too high? The West did not dare weigh progress in the balance; it already knew that the losses were real, but clung to the primitive human faith that a 'solution' – though unknown – would be found; a kind of blind arrogance. However, knowing that there *was* a debit side to development, it was disingenuous for the West to say, as it appeared to do: 'What is good enough for us is good enough for everyone else.'

Members of government present, and senior officials, showed no doubts. Did they hope to reap the immediate rewards of development and leave office before the social damage became too worrying – and dangerous?

Bill had remarked when our paths had recently crossed in Rome: 'Would any leader of an underdeveloped country dare tell the masses that some kinds of "progress" could be harmful? They'd tear him to pieces! Or simply wouldn't listen – they'd think he was out of his mind.'

In the world of *realpolitik* in which Bill played his 'great game', where politics and business were joined with higher, Byzantine reckonings, and the development industry spilled over richly into subsidised trade and industrial investment, questions of the common good were lost to view. Who really cared about the poisoned chalice? He himself had become uneasily aware of it; and though he had tried to dismiss it with an airy shrug as par for the course, the concern would not go away.

I marked each stay in Rome with a ritual walk through the old city – a mysterious homage to my journey from the Gorbals. There was a necessary stop before the Menorah carved on the inner face of the triumphal arch in the Forum, and the Moses of Michelangelo in S. Pietro in Vincoli. Why had those old stones, and Rome itself, become part of my quest, and a witness to it?

Werner kept an apartment in Rome, partly for business purposes, partly as a place to take a mistress – much more convenient on both counts, he said, than a hotel. As with Bill, we usually knew when we were both going to be in Rome, so that we could meet.

One evening we crossed the river to Trastevere and dined under a leaning tree in a little piazza by the river. Werner said he had been thinking of the significance of Rome for us both. We had often returned to that puzzle. From our table we could see the synagogue on the far bank, a white shimmer behind a row of trees. He said: 'Did you know that behind the synagogue is a convent where Jews were given papal protection? A stone above the gate says so. How effective that protection was when the Germans were here it would be interesting to know. That the refuge is there is ironic, when one remembers that Rome destroyed the Temple and scattered the Jews. I wonder if that is the true reason why we come here – to fathom why it all happened to us, then and since, and, in doing so, rediscover who we are. Remember *this* – in the fury of ancient times peoples were defeated and their cities and shrines destroyed, but the descendants of the survivors were not punished through the succeeding centuries as the Jews have been. Why have *we* been treated differently? Rome did a thorough job of crushing us. Why did later tyrannies feel the need to continue to set the wolves on what was left of us?

'Was it because we refused to fade away? Did they fear that their own faiths were not as strong as ours, and *that* fear fed their fury?

'Our faith *may* have questioned theirs. But not since the early days, at least not aggressively – and certainly not politically. True, we did not accept Rome's verdict and disappear – and still can't, though we've tried to fade into the host culture wherever we have been ever since the Enlightenment. Ah yes – *there's* an ironic word for you! What was enlightening about the last hundred and fifty years when you think of Rosenberg, Mendel Beiliss and the Nazis? Is it masochism that makes us come here looking for answers – like biting on an aching tooth? Do we still hope to settle accounts with the past? What can "settle" mean, at this late hour in history? Do we come here to ask ourselves if there is any hope? What hope could we look for after two thousand years?'

I said: 'You put your finger on it a moment ago. We come here to see clearly *what* we are. But why Rome? I wish I knew. Perhaps instinct is more accurate than we care to admit. Maybe we do expect the old stones to speak and give us answers.'

Whether Bill too found Rome a place for personal reassessment was less clear, but of late he probably did. He had lost the air of the happy buccaneer of earlier days. 'Sometimes,' he had said recently, 'there's a sour taste to this life I lead. I want to be free – to escape.'

'Where to?' I asked. 'To what?'

The blue eyes narrowed, and he shook his head once. He was aware only of an oceanic discontent, whether with himself or his vocation he would not say – or could not.

Early one May evening we met in a café in the Piazza Venezia. When he had telephoned to tell me he had arrived in Rome, he said: 'Let's meet under the historic balcony.' It took me a moment to grasp what he meant, the balcony of the Palazzo Venezia whence Mussolini had harangued the crowds in the Piazza Venezia at his feet. Before I could reply he changed his mind: 'No, as you were. Not there – I'll tell you why later. Let's meet at the café on the opposite side of the piazza – the one at the corner of the Corso.'

At the crowded tables at the pavement café, and in the throng moving round them, the air was electric, as if people would at any moment create the very excitement that spread out from them like palpable magnetism. He said: 'You can feel the tension, can't you? They wouldn't say it openly – well, some of them would, I suppose – but it's nostalgia for what that place meant in Il Duce's time. It is fashionable to meet under the *balcone storico*.' His nod took in the throng on the far side of the piazza, glimpsed through gaps in the frenetic traffic circling the piazza with horns blaring, and the breathless crowd passing to and fro near our corner table. 'In spite of the Italian Miracle, discontent is not far beneath the surface – in wistfulness for something missing – to equal the exaltation still glowing for them on that balcony.'

His sombre mood was out of keeping with his appearance, fastidiously turned out to project his professional self, as he called it, cream linen suit with not a crease in it, white shirt and dark-blue tie with its pale-blue diagonal stripe. But there were telling changes from the twenty-odd years since we had first met in Oxford. The fair hair receded, speckled with grey. The face was no longer tight of skin. There were wrinkles at the corners of the eyes. The signs must have made their appearance gradually, for this was the first time it had struck me that he no longer wore the gleam of youth.

He still contemplated the distant pavement, frowning now. 'They dream of bringing it all back. It's hard to believe. They really do.'

He spoke as if he knew some of the people milling about under the balcony. He glanced over his shoulder as Bernard often did, to see whether anyone was near enough to overhear, but the tables were full of vociferous young people intent on themselves. Young people! The thought brought me up short. How could the world have turned so fast?

He went on: 'What does that tell you about the way things are here, when it's not much more than twenty years since they hung Il Duce's corpse upside down in the street to be spat on?'

I was still asking myself how I could think of the people nearby as young – they were at least in their thirties! Ah yes! The words 'at least' said it all. Where *was* I, where were *we*, all of us?

He was looking at me questioningly.

I said: 'An unpleasant thought stopped me in my tracks: thinking all these people are – young!'

'What's unpleasant about that? They *are* young!' Then he looked shamefaced: 'You think it's *us*! I must admit the thought has crossed my mind recently.' He breathed through tightened lips. 'No, I'm not having that. The world really *is* as we see it. If we were too blind to see it before, that changes nothing. What I see over there *is* worrying.'

'You mean the packaging changes but the *people* don't!'

He thought about it. 'You're right, of course. The fact is, this game I've been playing all these years is showing its nasty side.'

The quiff of hair over his right temple lifted in the slight breeze, showing a loose flap of flesh. 'Come to think of it,' he said, 'how can one blame *anyone* for the mess the world's in? And blame's an odd word anyway – too trivial, like getting a bad mark at school for skimpy work on an essay! As if there's a top mark called "happiness" and we've missed getting it! Life's got to mean more than it does. On second thoughts maybe it *is* age – for all sorts of reasons.

'It's just struck me,' he went on, 'that the most personal things I did were for show, or to prove something to myself, with no emotional significance – women, for instance.' He made a face. 'That makes me sound damned emotionless, doesn't it? Which isn't me at all. There's a whole cargo of emotion waiting to be unloaded, and I wonder what stopped me before. God knows whether it's too late now. It was so simple to live for the day. You're right – age does come into it. I *have* been wondering where life has gone.'

I said: 'The facts haven't changed. It's *us*. When I think of trying to stop the world changing for the worse, I wonder why I didn't see how bad things were before. And yet I thought I was seeing things so clearly.'

He looked grave. 'I've never talked much about what I do. There are some very big projects. Deals for all kinds of equipment – never mind what they are – some of it in countries that haven't the foreign exchange to pay for it. Which means they're open to the influence that lending money gives; and if that doesn't bring the right answers, there's unpleasantness.' He shrugged. 'It's unstoppable.'

Bill had always seemed fully in control, moving the pieces in the great game with relaxed assurance. Now he saw that he himself was one of the pieces being moved.

We walked to the river and crossed to dine at the Galeassi in Trastevere, where the tables were wide enough apart, and there was enough background noise in the piazza, for us to talk freely. The swifts wheeled with a rustling of paper wings against the sapphire sky, and it was tempting to forget the threatening world.

He said: 'Some things one wants to change are immoveable, as if one were trying to shift the orbit of the earth. I once thought I had the answers – now I know I haven't. And it's not the kind of game you can just walk away from. I've no idea what I would do with freedom, apart from an immediate burst of pleasure, drinking and lazing in the sun and lust with young women – and when I tired of that . . . good God, I'm admitting it already! Yes, I *would* tire of it.

'And that's depressing. Age doesn't leave you alone, but one thing is sure: it doesn't improve you. Freedom would soon lose any meaning – no beginnings and no ends, no victories to strive for. They say that freedom means time to be fully yourself – and that's a terrible thought, for it means you haven't been yourself before! And who *am* I? Who was I *ever*? You know, I never asked myself *why* I was doing what I did. It was the *game* that mattered.'

At development conferences it was at first hard to believe that no one wanted to see their role as transferring to the Third World the social malaise of the West to add to their own. Bill had reached the right verdict upon his 'great game'– though how long he had lived with that self-knowledge I could only guess; it must have been many years. His reference to 'equipment' could have a very broad meaning, but in the context of Third World tensions and rivalries the significance was lamentably clear.

I thought of his image of trying to shift the orbit of the earth. Suppressed voices seemed to plead: 'We mean well! Let no one doubt it!' The political quicksands held *him* in thrall too.

My argument was that avoidance of social damage in recipient countries should be the starting point of aid policy, not a cosmetic concern when the damage became dangerously plain. Slowly, very slowly, people in the development industry, and in governments, began to admit that development might not be socially neutral after all. That was a start. Change in policy came more slowly.

I began to see, in wonder, that the roots of my campaign must have been laid in the Gorbals. Precisely *when* the process began, in flickers of light, visions of human discordances, is a mystery; the marvel remains. The acute awareness of childhood had seen far beyond immediate sensibility, and worked upon the vision in awed secrecy through the years. When I came to write the prize essay, I must have been shocked by the thought that to speak of 'answers' to anything in the human condition was to expect too much. How could you know what it was to aim too high? In the years after I left the Gorbals, when I was intent upon redefining my identity in the developed world to which Oxford introduced me, I must have pondered Gorbals parallels unawares.

Some Western attitudes, transferred innocently to the Third World, did not help matters. As a guest in the home of an American aid official in Africa, I was unexpectedly reminded of a persistent Western response to the dark continent: primeval, instinct with darkness of the blood. My host invited me to go hunting with him. He talked of the allure of killing. His appearance did not suggest the stock Hemingway figure of the great outdoors with a gun, but rather the urban man in grey flannel suit with a briefcase, fulfilling the aspirations of businesses.

His wife, a compact, smoothly assured woman with the demeanour of a long-practised stoic, murmured: 'He needs to kill things, which is really why we're living here at all.'

He grinned and gave her a playful nudge, and said to me in a tone of great seriousness. 'I really and truly feel it's important to kill something now and then, about once a month, maybe oftener sometimes. It keeps the natural instincts in balance, with nothing suppressed, and that's important. We were all of us hunters once upon a time, weren't we?' He thought about it and turned to her: 'Dear, it *is* about a month since I went out with my gun?'

She shrugged and smiled at him and said nothing.

He turned to me again: 'Yes, I can tell it's about time. I can't explain the feeling; something inside me knocking at the door, wanting to be listened to. When I get back each time, I feel renewed – as if something's been set free.'

I had forgotten Africa's image as one of the few remaining regions where Westerners could express aggression without guilt and in relative safety, live out fantasies of a life without restraints, of conquest, superiority; where élitism could be bought cheaply – in the footsteps of the Happy Valley expatriates and the rest. The safari industry in its many variations sold packaged simulations of the old adventurer days, bringing the frontier with the wild close enough to spice the experience. I wondered whether anyone stopped to reflect upon the moral effect on some Africans of seeing their land – and themselves in some contexts – marketed as a theme park, the elements of it bought cheaply from its poor populations. Certainly such business brought employment directly and indirectly, but the human costs must be real too, though hard to specify and measure.

In the long turbulence after the end of colonial rule in Africa, power, and the sometimes savage competition for it, brought no solutions – if that was the right word – only personal or sectional gains, usually transient. Something of the kind had been predicted long before the colonial flags were hauled down. With few exceptions Africa remains a region of deep suffering.

General Wassou had reminded me that since it was in the nature of military power to seek quick and decisive answers to instability, it was ill-advised to attempt long-term civil solutions on their own. Even in the most favourable conditions the army could only hope to be the arbiter of last resort – a reserve power, as he put it – necessarily guided by expediency, benevolent according to its lights, answerable to its own pragmatic judgment of the moment:

> *So spake the Fiend, and with necessity,*
> *The tyrant's plea, excused his devilish deeds.*

General Wassou was not the Fiend, far from it. He was a man of exceptional vision. He saw that he was constrained by the very absolutism of the power he represented. The Fiend was the blinkered optimism of the age of progress, allied to ubiquitous factional interest. In the inescapable power conflicts, each faction claimed that it alone could deliver progress without the poison – and from that multiple tug-of-war of interest no army could remain detached for long.

FIVE

Curtains of Dust

IT WAS SAID OF DESERT NOMADS THAT IF A FAMILY WAS GIVEN A new concrete house they would go on living in their black tent and use the house, if at all, for their livestock. The story expressed official frustration with nomad rejection of progress. It had been hard to believe. A government official offered to show me proof. Plainly, the planners regarded nomad peoples with unease as a law unto themselves, who posed awkward questions about the inadequacies of settled existence, its threat to traditional life. In offering modern accommodation and, in time, other services, the government hoped to entice nomads to join the rest of organised society. As to the damage this process would inflict on the nomad's way of life and his culture, the very question was a sign of 'backward' thinking, best ignored. That way of life had to give way to progress. Here was a classic confrontation: on one side the state trying to absorb nomads into settled social units with predictable behaviour – to say nothing of easily measurable taxable capacity; on the other the nomads defending their traditions as of greater value than anything the state could offer.

The gibe about using the new house for livestock recalled the

Gorbals, and a conventional boss class response to agitation for better housing: 'It would be a waste of good money. If we gave the tenement folk modern houses, they'd only use the bath to keep their coal in!' – which the Party dismissed as an insulting excuse for refusing to improve the condition of the poor. Bernard at his street corner meetings demanded evidence to support the boss class slander of the poor, but admitted to me privately that even if evidence *was* forthcoming it was irrelevant to the issue. It might simply show that some people clung to the old family ritual, warm and close, of washing in a galvanised iron tub on the kitchen floor in front of a coal fire.

In the jeep with the official and his driver I wondered if this search for evidence would also be vain. The driver was having difficulty fixing landmarks in the vast, almost featureless emptiness of sand and pale-brown rock, an implacable continent hurling indifference in our faces. Even if he found the house, the nomad family might have struck camp and gone; they might be anywhere beyond the wind-sculptured dunes on the horizon.

We found the house, a cube of concrete casting a long shadow in the slanting sun, in a hollow behind a line of dunes where patches of scrub betrayed the presence of water. Close beside it a sprawling black tent crouched like a bulky animal asleep in the sand. The official was about to drive straight up to it and give me a demonstration of recalcitrant attitudes, but at my suggestion we retreated a short distance along the way we had come, to where a low dune sloped down into the sand – a polite separation. From the further side of the tent a wisp of smoke snaked upwards. There was no need to intrude further.

The scene took the imagination beyond the features the official had criticised, obstinacy, backwardness, ingratitude. What harmonics of the spirit were at work in that dwelling-place, demanding to be left in peace?

I thought of the Romans, and the chain of concrete water cisterns they had built along the North African shore, some still providing fresh water for land and people and beasts. I had visited one, and tasted the water, cool and fresh in the echoing chamber. How sad that this inspired achievement had failed to halt the erosion of a vast fertile zone into desert. Could any form of progress bring it all back, a compromise between the interests of pastoral wanderer and settled cultivator? The black tent spoke eloquently; the concrete house did not provide such a compromise. Some missing quality needed to be found.

Near Bourg el Arab I was shown an experimental plot of a few acres, tightly fenced off from the desert, that had been irrigated regularly – force fed with water. Within the fence was a grove of trees and shrubbery and grass, a strong, defiant growth drawn out of a re-established top-soil. This was what the Romans had striven to preserve. A miraculous vision opened up, of such resurrected richness stretching all the way along the Mediterranean littoral as in olden days. It could still be done. Here was proof.

There were times when the desert questioned one mercilessly, more so in the deathly silent region further west, where high dunes shut away the sea, and no birds flew and no other sounds of life were heard, where no pretence or self-delusion could survive. At such moments the desert made it plain that it was certainly not neutral. I had a sudden perception of the magnetism of empty distance in the sea beyond the dunes that had beckoned Ulysses further and further, towards truths that relentlessly retreated. With just such an impression of limitless emptiness the desert erased all sense of direction, all certainties. I had discovered the sensation of a complete absence of bearings once before, in a desolate area north of Karachi, a little way inland from a rocky bathing beach frequented mainly by expatriates, with the perhaps ironic name of Paradise Bay. Leaving the sea's edge I had walked inland through hummocks of sand and rock and found myself in seemingly limitless desert with a scattering of similar hummocks some distance away in every direction. I was tempted to explore them but checked myself, certain that once among them, indistinguishable from the others, I might wander for ever. The sense of unremitting negation was so strong that although I had gone only a short distance from the invisible sea, I might have been miles from it. Quickly, before reason could leave me entirely, I turned about and retraced my steps and left that wilderness of burning sand with the strong feeling that I did so not a moment too soon.

Back at Paradise Bay, near a group of concrete beach-houses perched along a broken cliff-top, I sat on a rickety chair in the shade of a tarpaulin stretched on two poles from the side of a truck, where a lean old man in a long grey shirt and baggy trousers and sandals, who as far as I could see was the only other human being in this fiery wilderness, sold me a can of chilled Seven Up – welcome, as any cold drink would have been, in the nearly incandescent shimmer of heat. No sooner had I drained it than I was parched again, much to the man's delight – and I drank can after can. On the luminous Prussian Blue sea nothing moved. The horizon cut sharp along the edge of the sky and shut off the world. The sun's rays bounced off the white cement of the nearest beach-house, hard as a heliograph beam, and pierced the brain. My head drummed and echoed; I felt that it had been forcibly emptied in that brief stay in the crucible of the desert, and now demanded to be filled again. As the flurry of returning thoughts tumbled in, I asked myself whether this burning oven of land, beautiful and terrible in its barren purity, could once have been fertile. Would human inspiration one day make it flourish again?

I wondered, too, how the intuitions of that child in the Gorbals could possibly have been hurled forward to this day. The exaltation of that childhood magic returned. Of course it was possible. The sense of it was so potent that it could have been yesterday. There could be no doubt that this present white-hot sensitivity, here on the shore of the Arabian Sea, had come to me from those far-off days.

At the Sind Club in Karachi one evening I joined a young army officer and his wife for drinks and a swim in the pool. When he suggested meeting at sundown I must have shown surprise. 'It's the best time,' he said. 'The heavy heat of the day is over, and swimming is more refreshing. You will see.'

At our table by the pool, his wife remarked with a little wistful sigh, referring to an acquaintance at another table: 'She's so fair, isn't she?'

I was puzzled. The woman referred to had dark hair, almost black. In the nick of time I saw that 'fair' referred to the woman's *skin*. I was to hear 'fair' used in that sense again and again in the sub-continent. Fairness of skin was obviously important. Here was a clue to the preference for swimming in the dark, to prevent the sun's rays making one less 'fair'.

Under the dark-blue velvet sky, light from the submerged pool-side lamps combined with that from the club's windows to cast mysterious shadows in the water; and swimmers were dark rounded shapes above the wavelets. Everyone was 'fair' in the darkness. Here was an inversion of the sun culture of the West, to fit the preferences of a quite different culture: not sun worshippers but sun *avoiders*. This was in the mid-1960s, before the wider spread of concern about the thinning of the ozone layer and the risks of skin cancer in exposure to the sun.

In the West, the fashion of sun worship, encouraged by naturism and related movements in the 1930s, had become a passion to achieve a skin colour approaching that of people born with dark pigmentation – a reaction to an older culture that saw weathered complexions as lower class. To serve this new sun religion, there had arisen great industries selling 'sun' chemicals and related home appliances – a market swollen in the expansion of mass travel to sun-baked beaches – so that Westerners could attain the skin colour of people who wished *they* themselves were 'fair'! What did naturally dark-pigmented people of the Third World think of sales promotion that encouraged fair-skinned people to believe that their identities would be elevated by becoming as brown as possible? Amid such confusion how could anybody see anything clearly?

In my house off the Murree Road at Rawalpindi, I had a cook-bearer, Miraz, an ex-soldier of formidable physique, attentive, correct, a nice man. He had limited English, but with the few words of Urdu I picked up, I managed – just.

Foreigners were advised to hire a *chowkidhar* – night watchman – as well as a house servant, for additional security. I did so, though what my *chowkidhar*, a man long past his first youth, could have done if faced by an armed intruder was doubtful. Men came in from the hills with rifles slung, bandoliers across the chest, knives in view, a common sight. Some of them, according to a bank manager, came to him to deposit cash and gold. No questions were asked. He had even taken in gold Maria Theresa dollars, and wondered how many years they had been hoarded, and in what circumstances they had been obtained, up there on the frontier.

One night before going to bed I went out on to the porch to look at the stars. The *chowkidhar* was in the habit of squatting in the front doorway, and for all I knew slept there. He was nowhere to be seen. I called Miraz and asked him if he knew where the *chowkidhar* was. I had realised early on that they were not friends, and I now sensed that Miraz was not concerned about what had happened to him. My guess was that he had either not turned up or had fallen asleep at another bungalow where he had duplicated his employment as night watchman. Miraz, hovering in the corridor leading from the kitchen, must have divined my thoughts. He came up and said in his quiet, firm voice: 'Do not worry, Sahib, I have this.' He produced the biggest jack-knife I had ever seen and snapped open a blade about an inch wide and six inches long. He bent down and picked up a leaf from the step and with a hiss of the blade cut it in two as with a razor. He said: 'You see – I am here, with this.'

I said: 'Be careful with that. You might get hurt.'

He smiled gently and in one movement snapped the great knife shut and tucked it away. 'No, Sahib, no *me* get hurt.'

'Anyway,' I said, 'be careful.'

In that exchange a certain understanding must have been established.

The *chowkidhar* made his appearance the next night full of complaint that I did not trust him, implying that he *had* turned up but that I had not spotted him. I said I would like to be able to trust him.

He looked at me with the distress of the misjudged. Turning to Miraz, he gave vent to a tirade plainly aimed at me. Miraz, who like many large and muscular men moved delicately and fast, was at his side at once and spoke softly in his ear. All complaint ceased.

That was soon after my arrival. There had been delays in carrying out the Ministry's instructions to install a telephone in my house; and as I was some distance from anyone I knew, I think I was more concerned then about security than later on.

The next day I nearly lost Miraz altogether. The district had recently been connected to the Sui natural gas pipeline, and new gas cookers were being distributed and installed. Mine may have been faulty, or wrongly connected. I was waiting for breakfast to appear when there was an explosion in the kitchen at the back of the sprawling bungalow, followed by a deep-throated cry of pain. I found Miraz slowly getting up from the stone floor. He had a black scorch mark across his cheek, and looked in shock. The top of the cooker, a heavy casting, had been blown across the room where it had made a gash in the cement wall. Had it hit him, he could have been killed.

The floor was littered with utensils and bits of food. I found the main gas tap in the wall and turned it off, then took him by the arm and led him to the veranda and sat him down. From my first-aid training long ago, I remembered that hot sweet tea was good for shock. But with the cooker wrecked I had no means of making tea.

I wondered how devout a Muslim he was, and whether in any case I could risk giving him whisky. In my concern I could think of nothing else. I said: 'I know you must not drink alcohol, but I must give you something quickly. Will you drink some whisky?'

The broad frame in stained khaki shirt and trousers remained slumped in the chair, great hands resting on knees, jaw drooping, eyes staring at nothing.

'Can you hear me?' I said. 'It is important. You must let me help you – will you drink some whisky?'

My scruples might be unnecessary, but I had to know.

He looked up at me questioningly, then with a helpless shrug nodded as if past caring. I poured a decent measure of Scotch. He seized the glass and gulped down the contents. A convulsion shook his huge frame and faded. He gave a weak grin and slumped again.

I said, 'I am going to take you to the hospital and get the doctor to have a look at you. I'll help you into the car.'

As I drove to the Military Hospital, which as far as I knew was meant for officers and certain categories of officialdom, I wondered about the details of rank and protocol that sometimes tripped one up. There were curious glances from other cars; was it because Miraz looked so ill, or had I broken a convention in sharing my car with a servant? If the latter, so be it; there was no other way. When I drove through the hospital gates and explained that it was Miraz, not I, who needed attention there were doubtful glances. Luckily, a medical officer I knew slightly from the club drove up. He said he would look at Miraz himself.

I told him I had given Miraz whisky, in case that might conflict with any medication he might want to give him. I got a wink in return but no comment. I went outside and sat in a long chair on the dusty veranda, and reflected on how easily the rules were made, or bent, for some people. More to the point, how easy it was to accept privilege when it was there for the taking, as I was doing.

The doctor joined me. Miraz had been lucky. He was suffering from shock and a superficial burn to the face. He was coming out of shock, and the burn should heal quickly. He was silent, looking up at the sky with half-closed eyes. The early-morning sunlight, though diffused by the constant curtain of dust, spread a certain purity, which would fade under the main heat of the day. 'This is the best time,' he said. 'I think that's why I don't mind this early shift.' After another silence he added with a sigh: 'Do you know what the average expectation of life is in this country? It's about thirty-six for men.' He seemed about to say more, but stood up: 'I must get on with my round.'

A little later Miraz emerged holding himself erect, eyes bright again, a dressing on his cheek. He came to attention before me. 'Thank you, Sahib. They fix me all right.'

A few days later, Friday morning, Miraz said, with his usual formal politeness, that he needed to go to his village in the hills to help his wife with some problems. Would I permit him to be away for two nights? He would be back on Sunday evening at seven o'clock.

This was far from convenient. The replacement cooker was temperamental. I was still not confident about the *chowkidhar*. I was also extremely busy. For a moment I toyed with the thought of getting another cook-bearer – reminding myself that both locals and foreigners were casual about changing servants. I dismissed the idea – I had no time for the tiresome details, and in any case nothing would happen quickly enough. From his expression I saw that he must have guessed these thoughts, and I hoped my guilt did not show. I said: 'Do you promise – really *promise* – to be back here on Sunday evening?'

He ran his forefinger across his throat: 'Sahib, I promise – it is a sure promise.'

I waited for him to add 'Inshallah' as most locals did, at any level, equivalent to 'DV', God willing – a talismanic utterance, an insurance against breaking a promise, or perhaps against the temptation to break it. He looked me in the eye, his thin moustache straight, and said softly: 'For what you did, Sahib, I will not fail.'

The weekend passed quickly enough. I ate at the club. The dining-room was usually quiet. In a nearby room one could stretch out in a long chair for a nap afterwards.

On Sunday the weather was blustery. A black sky came down from the mountains, and from time to time storm rain came beating down, increasing in force towards evening till it battered the bungalow with the noise of hundreds of tiny hammers. I thought: 'He'll never get down from the hills in this.' I tried to concentrate on work at my desk, but as often happened in the district there were electricity failures, and more frequent than usual, presumably because of the storm. I thanked my stars I had plenty of candles and an oil lamp.

Seven o'clock came and went. The storm was worse. The electricity went off again. I heard a new noise at the back of the house. I picked up my torch and got to the kitchen just as the light went on again. Framed in the doorway was a figure that might have just walked out of the sea, draped in an old army greatcoat that dripped the almost liquid air straight down on to the step. From under the greatcoat his wet face peered out: 'You see, Sahib, I am here!'

I had heard no vehicle come up the quiet side road. He had obviously walked a considerable distance in the sheeting rain. He said he was sorry to be late, and would at once prepare my evening meal.

I never asked him what had been the business that had demanded his presence in his village. I told myself that I should have been more intuitive and guessed; Miraz must have been still in his thirties, and his wife probably considerably younger. It was easy to be infected by expatriate indifference.

One day in the hot weather, turning off the Murree Road into the road leading to my house, I saw Miraz at the corner with a figure in a white *burqua* – the all-enclosing woman's garment with a fabric visor in the helmet-shaped headpiece. Even through the loose folds it was plain from her movements that she was slim and young. A large covered basket rested at her feet. The sunlight glinted off the stones of the low wall at the side of the roughly surfaced road. The soft earth at their feet had dried into a fine white powder, some of which must have been whirled up by a sudden zephyr on to his shirt and trousers, turning them white too. The two white figures were stilled as in a primitive pastoral.

I drew up and he came over to the car. 'It is my wife, Sahib,' he said, though I had not asked.

'Do you want a lift to the house?'

'Yes, Sahib. It is hot.' He turned and called out to her in Urdu, and the sealed headpiece of the *burqua* nodded. He came round to the passenger door and got in.

'Isn't your wife coming?' I asked.

'She will walk to the house,' he answered, and closed the door.

I looked round and saw the concealed figure lift the basket with an effort, for she moved with one shoulder dragged down, and began to walk slowly after us. It was only about two hundred yards to my house, but in that enclosed garment, in that grilling heat, it must have been exhausting to walk at all, let alone carry any weight. However, it was part of the given. The whole performance was important. Certain ways of doing things supported hidden values, which in turn protected an entire inscrutable structure.

It seemed that all rituals were concerned with self-preservation, naturally imposed, even among the very young, where it was the most poignant. An extreme example was a 'tax' for the protection of cars, levied by a group of children. Foreigners talked of stolen hub-caps, side mirrors, anything detachable – significantly, one heard of very few thefts from locally owned vehicles. 'A nuisance, of course, but all you have to do is go into the bazaar and buy a replacement – most probably you would be buying back the bit of your car that was stolen! Still, that's how things are.'

It was hard to believe, like the story that 'persons unknown' steamed off stamps from outgoing letters and resold them. It was confirmed, however, by the existence of a counter at the post office where you handed your stamped letter to an official who cancelled the stamp in your presence, making it impossible for it to be re-sold as new. As for the stealing of attachments to cars, I ignored the warning till one day I stopped outside the post office, in a little square where hollow-cheeked old men – or younger men who *looked* old – sat cross-legged on the ground with old typewriters before them, ready to draft letters and type them on demand. A group of about a dozen children rose up round me, ranging in age from about seven to fourteen, most of them barefoot, laughing but watchful. The oldest greeted me politely: 'We will protect your car, Sahib. We do not want you to have any trouble. Anywhere in Pindi we will see to it. It is a promise.' He paused gravely, and the attention of the others flickered over me with gimlet eyes.

'How much?' I asked.

At once the group relaxed. The leader replied: 'The coins in your pocket – when we first see you each day. But we will be there all day, wherever you are. That is also a promise. If one day the money is less,' he shrugged and made a characteristic gesture of the hand, the wrist bent back and palm rotated with fingers spread, 'the next day you will have more. We will trust you.'

I took out the coins I had in my pocket, a few rupees and smaller coins and held them in my open palm for them all to see as they crowded round. The leader nodded but made no move. I said: 'Here is all I have. Take it. But tell me, how will you protect my car *wherever* I am?'

He looked first at his little followers and they all smiled happily: 'We have always known where you are ever since you came. No one will hurt your car. We will see to it. Now, Sahib, may I take the money? I want that all shall see.'

'Yes,' I said. He lifted each coin from my hand as in a sacred ritual, held it for them to see, and put it into a leather pouch slung on a broad belt under his long grey shirt, where I spotted the hilt of a knife protruding from a squat scabbard. As soon as he had finished, as if a spell had been cast, they vanished. I thought I saw one of the younger children in a doorway a few yards away. I watched for a few minutes, and saw another, a little older, come up to him and hand him a large lump of bread and disappear.

I went into the post office to have the stamp on an envelope franked. When I came out a few minutes later I found the young boy polishing a hub-cap on my car; it did not need cleaning – he was demonstrating that the car was under the group's protection. For the rest of my stay in Pindi, wherever I stopped the car one or two of the group rose up out of the ground to greet me, and each day a handful of coins changed hands. As an insurance policy, my investment did what I wanted of it. Nothing was stolen, nor was the car scratched or damaged. As for the cost, there was no way of knowing whether I would have been better off letting bits of the car be stolen and buying them back in the bazaar; I think compassion tipped the balance, as well as a certain admiration for the boys. Whether or not the enterprise was initiated by adults in the families concerned or by the children on their own account, I never discovered, and I suspect I did not want to; the poignancy, a certain charm too, might have been weakened.

Sometimes the world erupted in a fashion no forethought could have guarded against – always with significant lessons. One morning I drove along the empty Murree Road towards the centre of town, the air just beginning to lose the early freshness that would soon give way to the furnace heat of the high sun. Though this was a main road, like all the others it was curtained in dust – historic dust, centuries old, the dust of memory and forgetfulness. It was quiet, too quiet. I forgot that the impression of peace often meant the opposite. I thought ahead to an important meeting at the office later in the morning. Suddenly all semblance of peace vanished. Less than a hundred yards ahead, filling the whole width of road, a solid wall of people advanced fast towards me carrying banners and shouting slogans about justice and freedom. The sense of menace, of possession, vibrated towards me, a human tidal wave capable of destroying anything in its path.

In that instant, the first impulse was to turn the car and drive back the way I had come – and then find a detour to take me into Pindi from another direction; but I rejected it. I had not yet explored the 'back country', and this was not the moment for experiment. Besides, I was not sure I had time to turn about and accelerate away, and I had heard that such a move in front of a mob was likely to provoke it to violence in an outburst of thwarted anger. There had been several riots recently. My next thought was to drive on and hope the crowd would let me pass through – which was just as bad, and probably worse, than trying to escape. I decided on a third alternative, really the only one left, to stay where I was, and show that I was a neutral spectator. I swerved sharply and mounted the low kerb and stopped between two trees in the row lining the road, switched off the engine and put the keys quickly into an inner pocket, and sat back and lit a cigarette, hoping I looked relaxed.

They were drawing level with me. Seeing me stop and get out of their path, there was a momentary hesitation in the front rank; then it surged on while a young man detached himself from it and ran over to me. He looked in at the driver's window, sending out waves of tension as if he must deliver a challenge at any cost. He was dressed in the typical long grey shirt and baggy trousers, and wore a flat round cap of black caracul fur. I drew on my cigarette in silence, and tried to convey the impression that I was happy to wait. The suspicion in his eyes changed to impatience. He glanced round and I could see that he was upset that the mob was leaving him behind. He seemed to remind himself that he ought to say something to match the rioters' tension. Sharply he said: 'Where are you going?'

'To work,' I answered. Something about the way he surveyed the car, the only one of its kind in Pindi, told me he knew it, and probably knew what my work was.

His expression changed. He wanted to show that we were both in the grip of circumstance. He leaned on the window frame and said in a tone almost of comradely concern: 'You be careful.' He nodded in the direction I was heading. 'They are burning buses down there.' He ran off, presumably to resume his place in the leading rank, already a little distance along the way I had come.

Ahead, the road was now empty. I started the engine and eased the car down the step of the pavement on to the road and continued into the town and to my parking place at the Secretariat. One of the young protection group materialised and pocketed my handful of coins. He scrutinised the car as if he expected it to have come to some harm. 'Sahib, did you not know we are having a riot this morning?'

He could not have been more than nine or ten, and already he spoke in world-weary tones. 'Having a riot' sounded like 'having a party'. And to say 'we' meant that *he* was part of it – raised to the role of full participant in the grown-up world. His solicitude was real.

I shook my head and smiled acknowledgment. His young forehead wrinkled in concern. 'But, Sahib, you must be careful!'

I wondered what he would grow up into. In truth he was not a child any more. I thought of myself at his age; I understood how he felt, he and all the others. The child's thin form was but a mask. Within, as I remembered very well, he was doing what he could to lift his head above the parapet of the adult world.

He looked puzzled, seeming to ask what it was my smile acknowledged in him. I wanted to tell him, but he would not have understood. I was not sure I understood it myself. It was hard being his age, as part of me would never forget.

He turned and paced purposefully up and down beside the group of parked cars, proclaiming possession and challenge, his bare feet leaving firm prints on the sandy ground. This patrol was for my benefit too. Everyone played a game of some kind, maintaining position, status, acting in a chosen character, as this little fellow plainly was – or rather a designated character, for they too had no choice, as I had had none at his age. These children were learning fast, too fast. There was no way of telling him so; and even if there was, what could he do about it?

Sometimes, remembering Miraz showing me the fearsome knife he carried, I saw how close to the margin of life many people here lived. I wondered how Miraz would respond if I myself needed help – not in the way of using that knife but in dealing with some practical crisis.

During the hot weather something of the sort did happen. Intestinal and stomach attacks were common experiences, but I had escaped them so far. One day, on my usual visit to the club in the middle of the day for a pint of iced water and lime, I felt very tired and got up to leave and was so weak I had to sit down again. I should have remained there instead of driving home; at the club, medical officers could quickly be summoned, if none was at the usual concourse at the bar. But I had important papers to look at, and made the mistake of thinking that the weakness in the legs and nausea and a fierce headache were due to the heat and would soon pass. I was distantly conscious of making my way to the veranda and across the compound to my car, the sun falling like a hammer blow on my neck; and in a half-dream – really very unwisely – driving to my house and negotiating the gateway into the driveway, the latter a tricky manoeuvre even when in my right mind. How I got from the car into the house was a complete blank. My next moment of awareness was of seeing the ceiling and the sensation of lying on a stone floor – in the corridor where I must have collapsed – and Miraz looking down at me with furrowed brow. I tried to get up but discovered I had no strength; and I was in that remote state of mind in which it did not matter whether I got up or not. I must have lost consciousness again. I woke up lying on my bed, with two figures looming over me: the doctor who had treated Miraz at the Military Hospital, and Miraz himself standing a polite distance behind him. The air-conditioner rattled away, making a thudding noise inside my head, the room airless and dim with the blinds closed.

The doctor's voice seemed to come from far off. 'Ah, hello! That's better now. I've given you a shot. It'll soon pull you round. That's a nasty bug. I suggest you avoid ice for a bit. I'll come round later and give you another shot.'

I heard a groan and realised it had come from me. He laughed: 'Don't worry, you'll be all right soon' – and turned to put his impedimenta into a brown Gladstone bag. I raised myself on an elbow. He swung round to me at once. 'Hey – none of that! Lie down, old boy – give yourself a chance.'

I obeyed, and said: 'How did you know I was ill?'

'Your bearer got hold of me at the hospital – I don't know how. He said you were dying! I came right over. A good chap! Well, I must be off – I'll drop in and see you in about three hours' time. Don't eat anything – even if you feel like it!'

He turned to Miraz and spoke to him in Urdu – which I afterwards learned was to tell him to boil the water well, always to scald dishes and utensils and cutlery in freshly boiled water. I thought I had already given him those instructions; still, the doctor was issuing his orders as a matter of military routine.

The world was distant. Only the grey walls and the air-conditioner and the sweat-soaked bed clothes were real. Miraz went softly away. I slept.

I did recover quickly. The doctor, in the bluff style of his military calling, was impressed by Miraz's prompt action in summoning him. With a touch of British understatement and imagery still to be heard – though sometimes adopted in jest – he said that Miraz's prompt action had been a 'jolly useful thing'.

Apart from the cooker explosion, and the weekend off and the storm, I had had few exchanges of any importance with Miraz. He had little enough to do. He kept the bungalow clean and tidy, was attentive when I needed him, saw to my laundry, bought food – including *his* food, where he had a free hand – cooked simple meals. For the rest he enjoyed a kind of club life in the company of bearers from nearby houses in the enclave where I lived, Satellite Town. Their club room was a concreted area, a kind of patio between my house and the one next door, where in the evenings they sat and talked, and in the cool weather kept a log fire going in an iron brazier. That house had a telephone on a lead long enough to stretch out on to the patio, allowing the bearer to answer it without getting up from where he squatted at his back door. It had been through him, also an ex-soldier, that Miraz had contacted the doctor and told him I was dying. It was in the nature of Miraz: a resource, a depth of character, a reflective curiosity, an independence of mind such as I had often found in hill dwellers.

Later that day the medical officer remarked: 'Sound chaps, most of these ex-army fellows from the district. Pity there's not much else they can do when they come out of the army.' Miraz and the doctor had a link, though a tenuous one, in the army, in the clarity and predictability of power.

Power of another kind was demonstrated in an incident in Delhi that could have turned out disastrously. I was in the back of an official car being driven through a crowded bazaar area on the old airport road, with people drifting haphazardly from one side to the other – when my driver braked hard. I only just managed to grip the seat in front to stop myself crashing into it, and as I did so I caught sight of a grey-haired man apparently falling to the ground in front of the car bonnet. The crowd closed in menacingly, all eyes turned on *me*, not on my driver. I thought: 'A white face in a car that's just knocked down an elderly man! That's all I need.'

I tried to appear concerned but calm, and sat still. I glanced about for any sign of police, not unlikely for we must have been near the airfield, but saw none. Even if I had seen any, I might not have been able to attract their attention in time, across the hundreds of heads drawing closer on every side. My driver, a cheerful, confident young man, said over his shoulder, 'Sahib, do not worry! This will be all right. I will see to it.'

He switched off the engine and put the keys in his trouser pocket, threw open his door and got out deliberately, head erect, the image of confidence, even of arrogance, outfacing the people pressing on the car and banging on it. He paused for them to make way for him, then, as some were slow, roughly pushed his way through and round to the front of the car. I could just see the victim's head. The driver went up to him and looked him over, then pulled him to his feet and yelled at him to clear off: 'I know that old trick, pretending I knocked you over! Now get away from here. Go on! Shift!'

He added something in Hindi. He may have used English partly to emphasise a superior position, and perhaps, also, so that I should understand what he said. He stood with legs apart, hands on hips, facing the man.

To my relief the 'victim' showed no sign of injury. The man peered into my driver's face in affronted dignity mixed with appeal, then turned to the crowd for signs of support. He put his hand to his side with a grimace of pain, to show where the car had hit him. People near him in the crowd, now no longer a mob but a collection of casual spectators, shook their heads – it was thumbs down. My driver strutted even more eloquently. Power, the crowd must have concluded, lay with him, and they preferred to support the stronger side. The 'victim' turned away and was gone.

My driver glared at the sea of faces – in place of menace there was now admiration. Grinning, he strolled back to the car, the sun gleaming on his black hair and neat white shirt with white shoulder straps, a cut above them all. I breathed again. Back in the car he said:

'You see, Sahib, I told you there was nothing to worry about!'

It sounded as though he had been in such a situation before. His timing and judgement had been perfect. But it had been a near thing.

If his skin had been white, or if I myself had been driving, the outcome would almost certainly have been fatefully different – for of course the crucial element that had ended the crisis, a brutal dismissal of the victim, would have provoked violence.

I was tempted to ask him if he was sure the car had not hit the man, but decided against it. It would be letting him down, and myself too. In his display of power he had protected us both. But had it been fair?

Long afterwards, when I could describe the event without identifying the driver, I mentioned it to a middle-aged Indian friend of some rank. He said: 'Alas, my people are easily influenced by displays of power. Indeed it seems to reassure them. To give your driver the benefit of the doubt, he may have been right in judging it to be a try-on. Even if it wasn't, he understood his people well!'

'Either that,' I said, 'or he was relying on the fact that he was driving an official car – and his aggressive stance underlined it to the crowd. Power again?'

'Maybe,' my friend said. 'But either way, the wrong side won. If your driver *had* knocked the man down, he should not have got away with it – though in such a case *you* might well have suffered at the hands of the crowd also, probably quite badly. These things happen! And even if it *had* been a try-on, to respond to it with a display of "might is right" should not have won the day. But it did. And one must always regret it.'

The fact that power and its leverage was often unfairly used had obviously come his way many times. For him, as for so many others, it was par for the course.

SIX

Marooned

WHEREVER I WENT I SAW POWER RESPECTED, AND ATTEMPTS to manage affairs without it despised. Of course the Third World was not alone in this, but because of the extremes of hardship, of injustice, of hopelessness to be found there, where people were obliged to battle so much harder against circumstance, they seemed in a worse state than anywhere else. Yet the rich countries, spurred perhaps by feelings of historic guilt, believed they were doing all they could to improve the world, on the principle that poverty alone was the cause of all other evils. Was the sum of evil greater or less if poverty was reduced? How could I of all people ask such a question?

I thought of the gentle confidence of Mr Wolf and Bernard's father – that reason was the answer to everything and would always triumph in the end. In the *end*! Who could live long enough to put that to the test?

I was aware of a personal conflict in all this; on the one hand a feeling of concord with the sufferers, on the other a compulsion to stand back and look for 'reasons' – for in those early influences upon me the message was strong and clear – if you knew the *reason* for something, you had the answer! I was drawn back through the years to find the key to my motives for being in the Third World at all – fury with the world's inhumanity, its capacity for nurturing chaos, and in myself the continuing prayer to burst the bonds set upon me long ago. I was taken back to an experience where I was shut out in every sense, with no idea what to do to survive. To this day, when I think of it, the nerve endings are tender.

On a winter day – I was about nine – I came home from school and ran up the curved tenement steps and knocked on the door of our flat in light-hearted impatience, eager to hear Father's heavy tread approach and feel his touch on the inner handle and his strong hand pulling the door open. Instead there was silence on the other side of the door. In sudden fear I hammered at the door, asking myself for the first time in my life what I would do if he really was *not* there and never came back. I hammered till my knuckles hurt and blood oozed through the skin. The silence beyond the door remained. Frozen with oceanic fear, I stumbled down the stairs to the close mouth to peer short-sightedly at faces in the gathering dusk, as if my longing could conjure Father's stocky form from the passers-by and seize hold of his hand never to let it go. Again and again I went up the stairs and banged on the door – why, I could not have said, for if he *had* come home while I stood at the close mouth I would have seen him. Doubt had struck me senseless. I must have stood there for several hours in desperate fidelity, my eyes watering with the strain of staring, the cold from the flagstones creeping through my torn boot soles and up my legs, hunger biting into me, fear weighing me down like a sodden cloak, wondering what to do, where to go. I was tempted to go to Aunt Rachel and Uncle Zalman a few streets away, in defiance of Father's injunction not to visit them. I postponed that decision. I went to the gambling club a few minutes away across the river – a fearsome place with a heavy brown wooden door and a spy-hole in it, through which excited voices could be heard, and cigarette smoke filtered out on to the landing. Trying to hide my tears, I asked the giant of a doorman if Father was there. The contempt in his reply was like a blow on the face: 'Och, him! He went awa' skint a long time ago. Go on – hop it! It's against the law fer ye tae be here anyway.'

I trudged back, now so tired and cold it was painful to lift my feet, and climbed the cold staircase and banged on the door with the hand that did not hurt. In the silence on the other side of the door there was a demonic presence forbidding me to hope. Could Father have left me for ever? No, he *must* come back. If I went to my aunt and uncle, the very next moment he would return and be angry that I had gone. I went down to the close mouth and stood shivering with cold, trying to understand what it was like to be alone in the world.

The lamp-lighter passed slowly on his high bicycle and stopped at the next fluted lamp-post at the pavement edge beyond the close and reached up with the little hook at the end of his pole to move the gas tap at the base of the enclosing lantern until the mantle burst into pale-yellow radiance. How often had I watched him with envy, a figure of grace and magic? That was a long way in the past, together with everything else I had ever known. He was now a figure of doom, marking the passing of hope. Across the street in the baker's shop the lights shone tantalisingly on round brown buns on a shelf in the window, but I had no money to go over and buy one. I stamped my feet on the cold stone, and told myself I would count up to a hundred and then go to my aunt and uncle. I forgot the number I reached and stopped counting. The damp cold went through my bones, and my feet hurt. Fewer people passed. A dark figure approached, like Father in build, and my heart soared, but it was not he. As he came near I thought I knew his face from one of the closes nearby. He stopped and said: 'Laddie, ye've bin standin' there fer 'oors – ah kin tell somethin's wrong. Ye kin tell *me*. Ye know we live in the next close. We want tae help ye.'

I tried to speak steadily. I was waiting for my father. The man exclaimed: 'Yer feyther! He cannae have . . .' He checked himself.

Years later I understand why. Men sometimes disappeared from their families; and it was part of the local code to make no comment lest one be accused of 'interfering', and that could lead to bad feeling, and fights.

He said: 'Ah cannae le' ye stand there a' night. Ye look done in. Ye'd be'er come tae oor hoose, an' ma missus'll gie ye somethin' tae eat an' ge' ye warrm by the fire an' le' ye ge' some sleep. Anyway doan't ye fret. We'll find a way tae help ye in the mornin'.'

If I went with him, I thought, I would not incur Father's anger by going to my aunt and uncle. That was as far as my numbed mind dared reach. I looked behind me into the dark close and the stairs; maybe Father would materialise and save me? The stone cavern remained silent. There was no escape. As if I walked to Hades I followed him to a house in the next close. The kitchen, the same size as ours, pulsated with warmth from a bright fire in a polished range with steel edges burnished bright. A woman in a flowered wrap-round apron, fair hair drawn tightly back from a narrow, bulging forehead, reached out and held me close and spoke to the man over my head: 'The puir wean. He's a block o' ice! We should have got him in here before.'

He must have told her he had seen me waiting in the next close mouth and they had at first been fearful of 'interfering'.

She sat me on a stool by the fire and rubbed my hands in hers, then when the warmth from the fire had thawed me out led me to the table – of rough wood, and covered with cracked oil cloth like ours – and put a bowl of hot soup and a lump of bread before me. I ate automatically, taut with foreboding, wondering what Father would say – inwardly insisting to myself that he *would* reappear. I knew the man and woman were mouthing silent words at each other, and that they pitied me, which reminded me that my plight really was serious. I must have fallen asleep where I sat.

The next thing I knew it was morning and I lay wrapped in a grey blanket on the kitchen floor, near the grate, where the fire still glowed. As if opening my eyes had summoned them, the tiny kitchen was suddenly crowded with the family — the man and woman and a boy about my age in a green jersey and brown shorts and black boots, and a girl in a green dress and jersey and brown boots who looked younger. 'Who's this new yin?' they exclaimed.

The woman replied: 'He's frae the next close. He got locked oo' last night. Yer feyther's goin' tae take him back in a wee while.'

She gave me a mug of hot milk, and a white egg-cup with an egg just boiled. I was afraid to eat, suddenly guilt-ridden for having eaten what she had given me the night before, remembering now the Jewish taboo against 'trayfah', food not approved by the dietary laws, which also governed dishes and utensils. I still could not absorb what had happened, emphasised by my presence here with strangers. If I refused to eat I would have to explain why, but how could I interpret a 'law' I had followed without question since earliest memory? Besides, my rescuers might not believe me. They, too, I must have sensed, were trapped in an event beyond under-standing. I caught their sad looks at each other; I could almost hear them say: 'Poor boy, what are we to do?'

It struck me that I should protect Father from their thoughts, but *how*?

These riddles were swept away by what followed, which has remained vivid in my memory ever since; even now it seems demoniacally timed, an atrocious stroke of fate. When I levered away the top of the eggshell with the spoon, the flesh beneath was discoloured blueish yellow, and stank. I was seized with fear and sympathy; fear of their anger if I did not eat it, sympathy because I knew its condition could not be their fault. They were giving me what their poor resources could provide, indeed more, for I was the only one given an egg — the others ate bread and dripping with their tea. How could I tell them that what they had given in goodness and sacrifice was rotten?

I decided to force myself to eat it. I dug the spoon into the discoloured flesh but could not summon the will to take it to my mouth. The woman said kindly: 'Go on, laddie, an egg's guid for ye.' As she spoke she leaned closer, and with a cry seized the egg-cup with the egg in it and held it out to her husband: 'Look wha' the dairy man gave me! He gave me this for new-laid! Look wha' ah've jist given the puir wean! It's a disgrace! Go doon this minute an' gie 'im a right piece o' yer mind.'

Tight-lipped, face flushed, the man got to his feet, took the egg with one hand and his jacket from a hook behind the door with the other and rushed out. She turned to me, face crumpled in dismay, and I had an awesome impression, never to be forgotten, of the unfairness of life – you tried to do good and a malign power defeated you! She had guessed, rightly, that the egg confronted me as yet another dark omen – destiny emphasising my derelict state. She came round the table and touched my cheek: 'Ah'll boil ye a fresh egg the minute ma man comes back wi' i'. Aye, an' doan't ye worry. We'll find yer faither for ye.'

Her husband was soon back, red-faced from running up the stairs, and perhaps with residual fury from confronting the dairy man. He held the new egg, a brown one this time, at arm's length as if his whole being depended on its witness, and handed it to her with a frown, which she acknowledged with a lift of the chin; the egg had become a talisman. She lowered it into a shiny copper saucepan standing ready on the coal range and murmured: 'Ah cannae believe that dairy man didnae know! How could he dae a thing like that tae us? We're respectable folk! We doan't owe him money – well, no' since you've been in wurrk!'

She moved the saucepan to one of the round cooking lids on the flat top of the range and continued her protest: 'Ah wanted to dae ma best for the wean. Ah wanted tae gie him a special bi' o' love a' a time like this! An' then ah go an' gie him a rotten egg!'

Her words uplifted me, but it would be many years before I fully understood why. They reached out to me and turned away the hard edges of loneliness and perplexity and fear, held out a straw of redemption. The world was softened a little. Years later I often wished I could return to that moment and tell her that I understood what she had wanted to do, and remembered it always.

When the egg had boiled enough, she lifted it out of the pan in a tablespoon and stepped sideways to the shallow earthenware sink in the adjacent corner of the little room, held it under the tap to cool the shell, and brought it to me in the white egg-cup, with a thick slice of bread on a cracked plate. The boy and girl stared in puzzlement, their questioning suppressed by solemn signals from their parents. I was possessed by a chill need to discover what awaited me in the silent flat in the next close, and yet wished I could escape it. I ate quickly and tried to forget that I was the centre of attention.

Nothing more was said. The man and his wife seemed to share a moment's contentment, though behind it I felt their concern for me.

Many questions raced through my mind. Was I behaving correctly to these strangers? How soon could I decently leave them and go and look for Father? Would they really help me to find him?

The woman told the boy and girl it was time for school. That meant it was time for me to go too; I realised I still had my school satchel with me – and that brought back the shock of the day before, and especially the cold and hunger.

How could I go to school not knowing where Father was? The man put his teacup down with a little click of emphasis and turned to me: 'Laddie, when ye've finished yer breakfast ah'll take ye tae yer hoose. Yer faither's maybe wonderin' where ye are! Then ah've got tae go tae ma wurrk. If he's no' there ah'll bring ye back here an' ma missus'll decide what to do next. But don't ye worry. It's goin' tae be all right.'

The woman stood over the boy and girl while they washed their hands at the sink, clicking her tongue at them as if they were little animals, telling them to dry their hands properly: 'Ah doan't want ye gettin' chapped hands and chilblains!' She dabbed water on the boy's head and smoothed his hair down, then put a large comb through the girl's hair and pulled the hem of her dress straight.

Watching her, I felt an additional sadness – not that I consciously wanted her to pay such attention to me, but a feeling of remoteness returned, which I had experienced with crushing intensity the evening before when I had stood at the close mouth in the dark and wondered if I would ever see Father again.

Gently but firmly she pushed the boy and girl out of the kitchen, and seemed about to follow them out on to the staircase, but stopped in the doorway and called after them: 'Run along then!' Then she turned and reached out to me and smoothed my hair with both hands. Hesitantly she released me: 'Go on, laddie,' she said, with a tense smile. 'Go wi' ma man. An' doan't ye worry now. We'll stand by ye.'

I could not have said why that smoothing of my hair gave me an infusion of confidence. It brought a tear too. A host of impressions had thrown me about since the previous afternoon, demanding that I respond to the suddenly changed world without knowing what it wanted of me, imprinting one certainty only – the world would never again be as I had thought I knew it. Unbelievable things had happened. I had slept in a strange house – and not a Jewish one, a shattering event in itself – which with all the rest must surely change me. But how? I wished I knew, or that someone would tell me. If all was going to be in flux, how would I know *what* I was, what was real and what was illusion? Would I ever confront this newly revealed world without fear?

There was one slender reassurance. The man and his wife had conveyed a tiny measure of certainty, not enough to banish fear, but enough to push it away a little. I felt I should say something – there was so much to say, the words tumbling about in my head, eluding my grasp. I wanted her to know that I was too full of unmanageable emotion for *any* words to fit. She probably guessed. I looked up at her through my steamed spectacles, and muttered shakily: 'Thank you for – for – for helping me.' No other words would come. My satchel held tightly as if it contained life itself, I went out of their front door, wanting to look back and claim a little more of the warmth she had given me. I followed the man down the echoing stone staircase and into the bustling street. The world was suddenly too close. People stared into my face and turned away and whispered to one another. Were they saying: 'Why is he with that man who is not his father – and so early in the morning? Where *is* his father?' I did not know that these people had preoccupations of their own, and my state was of only passing interest to them. Perhaps I did sense it, and the knowledge made me fear the terrible new magic of the changed world all the more. If nobody cared then the world would always be ice-cold like this.

We went into our close. The tread of the man's heavy labourer's boots resounded in my head like the march of giants.

He knocked confidently on the door. There was silence. He banged with his fist and the little stone landing reverberated with the dull blows. Then came the sounds I had longed to hear all those hours before, Father's tread. They halted on the other side of the door as if to consider something – and my heart hammered and I was sorry that this stranger was at my side. Father opened the door. He was in trousers and woollen undershirt, braces hanging down. He stood blinking, then muttered: 'What time is it? I thought I would lie down for a minute, and then . . .' He looked questioningly at my companion. The man had begun to turn away the instant the door opened. He said: 'Ah've go' tae ge' tae ma wurrk,' then clattered down the stairs.

Father took me in his arms and held me tightly. I wept. I could not have said that I wept for him more than for myself but the thought was there – for he had just said something that filled me with anguish for him. The words 'What time is it?' told me he must have pawned his watch, a great fat silver hunter whose hinged lid had always fascinated me with the ringing *ping* that sounded when he pressed the button in the winding knob to make it spring open. His name was engraved in curly letters on the mirror-like inside surface of the lid, signifying that it was part of his very own magic kingdom. He had won the watch at the gambling club and with soaring optimism had had the engraving done. The watch must have signified a status he thought should be his always. To be forced to pawn it must have hurt him even more than parting with the majestic amber cigarette-holder ringed with gold that had gone the same way long before. A surge of terror greater than any I could remember went through me: had he hoped, this time, to sleep for ever? The thought did not mean *ever*, really ever, something I had puzzled over since mother had died, but something close to it, a loss that could not be recovered. The idea of finality did come to me then but slipped out of my grasp.

I felt a despairing sympathy for him, and shivered, for how could this be – he who was so strong and yet so vulnerable? That thought was too saddening to bear, and was banished. It returned years later, when I saw that he had been trying all the time so hard to attain a freedom of action he only partly understood but nevertheless wanted to pass on to me. It must have been *then* that he saw the sublime irony of his life, that he had been wounding himself over and over again chasing shadows, and in proof of it there I was, suffering with him, unprotected.

He said he had been asleep during all the hours I had feared him gone for ever. He had not heard my knocking on the door. He had been at the gambling club the whole night before that, and had come home in the morning just in time to give me breakfast and see me off to school, and then, being laid off work for the day, had gone to bed and slept on and on. Waking a little while ago and discovering my absence, a cold sweat had seized him. I was struck by life's propensity for caprice, the bizarre juxtaposition of events. While I had been trying to decide whether to eat the bad egg or to 'shame' my rescuers by telling them of it, he had been trying to make up his mind, with the immigrant's fear of officialdom, to go to the police for help in finding me.

And now, hearing the heavy banging on the door, he had thought it *was* the police, and had stood there in the darkness behind the door scourging himself with guilt, wondering how he would answer the humiliating and perhaps dangerous questions they would ask.

That must have been the first time I sensed the full bitterness of his lonely journey, and felt the burden falling on my shoulders and wondered at its great weight – my first moment of responsibility, too early by far. Guilt hit me hard then, *his* guilt, which must be mine too.

Could I have stored away that state of unmanageable desolation as guidance for the future – to resurrect it when I opposed the assumptions of the essay question: '*Has science increased human happiness?*' – and discovered that my answer was already written within me? And later still, decades later, it came to me that all curiosity, experiment, scepticism, the shape of any certainty I might find, were rooted in the sensitivity of childhood.

SEVEN

S. Giorgio's Bitter Fruits

IN THE 1960S AND 1970S THE EXPRESSION 'NEW WORLD ORDER' was much in the air at international conferences on development and in its literature. I thought at first that it could only be a pious hope for an ill-defined redemption. It seemed to envisage the world of the future *not* as a collection of potentially antagonistic peoples competing for the greatest material prizes – as it had always been – but as a family of mutually benevolent peoples wanting the *same* things, and co-operating so that all may gain them. The sole obstacle was inequality of consumer power. The vision appeared to ignore the claims of competing traditions, value systems, of power and aggressive identity as motivations – but that it was enough to recognise that all peoples were 'entitled' to the same fulfilments, which no one cared to define. What 'entitled' meant was not clear either. Was it Rousseau's 'general will' stretching over the entire world, granting – and presumably enforcing – that entitlement? Such a vision must include the ultimate goal of world government. In that light, development subsumed much more than alleviating particular deprivations, but a uniformly consumerist world – whatever the human cost in establishing it.

It did not grapple with the implication that for a world system to function it must have centralised power. Any 'permissive' world government would defy the Austinian warning that law without the sword is a contradiction in terms. Along that route, accordingly, how did one escape the high likelihood that *any* 'world order' would bring world tyranny? It was probably no accident that the term 'superpower' was also entering common usage at that time.

Images of the possible are matters for strife only because the supposed facts that people cling to and quarrel over are often not facts at all but fruit of the imagination. Norman Douglas – eloquent Italophile – speaks of this magisterially in *Siren Land*:

> What strange creatures we are, placing more faith in deductions than in facts – why? God created the facts and they may take care of themselves, but the deductions are our own, to be clung to with parental attachment.

But what *are* the facts? That question is usually unwelcome because it demands the uncovering of sensitive desires and motives – or too deeply hidden to be willingly drawn up into conscious thought; but it is in those depths that a people's view of life's aims is preserved.

To reach those depths I went to live in a village in a region not strictly speaking part of the Third World but nevertheless 'backward' according to received opinion – a community that belonged to an older European tradition, uneasy about the consequences of following the new consumerist world view that touched them from 'outside'. In Italy the *Mezzogiorno* is still sometimes spoken of as a forgotten country.

For nine months between 1975 and 1976, I lived in S. Giorgio Albanese, a *paese* of 1,800 people on a remote mountain ledge in the deep south of Italy, in Calabria in the 'foot' of Italy between the instep and the toe. Little more than a decade before, access to it had been by mule track. There on the extreme southern edge of Europe I found a culture whose 'backwardness' lay in fidelity to nineteenth-century ideals of identity and fulfilment.

Its people knew well enough that profound change was inescapably on the way, and that it was likely to be more damaging to traditions and hopes than any they had known before. Certain values would be lost or weakened on the way. Would the gains, if any, be worth the loss?

The word 'Albanese' in the name of the village, and in the names of other Italo-Albanese communities in Italy, partly explains why the past retained a powerful grip, through a rare conjuncture of chance and history. These communities are descended from bands of Albanians owing allegiance to Skanderbeg, who crossed the Ionian Straits in flight from the inroads of the Turks in the late fifteenth century, a flow that continued into the early years of the following century. They built fortified villages and went their own way, apart from sporadic conflict with the indigenous population. Their mother tongue to this day is Albanian, which they call *Arberesh*. Italian is the second language. Physically, too, there are differences: paler skin, fresher complexions, grey eyes. They retain the *rito greco* – follow Greek Orthodox rites – but under the authority of Rome, and have their own bishop at Lungro.

The mountains lean round tightly, the lower slopes supporting olives and vines, chestnuts and herbs. High behind the village to the south stretches the lonely immensity of the Sila, a mountainous region once heavily timbered, where there are still wolves. Immediately to the north the slopes tumble 1,700 feet to the fertile plain of ancient Sibaris, the *Piana di Sibari* – the *pianura* – and the meandering Crati that spills into the Gulf of Taranto. Further north is Monte Pollino, 7,500 feet, and the passes leading to Senise and the Carlo Levi country. Mountains shut away the horizon in a great curve from the south, leaving a 'window' at S. Giorgio Albanese looking down to the *pianura* and the remote outside world

– where one stood poised in mid-air on a platform before the church on the very edge of the ledge. Whenever I went there to look 'out', I thought of it as the Windowsill.

A telling illustration of 'out', as the S. Giorgesi understood it, was driven home early in my stay. Meeting someone – anyone – in the piazza, one might ask where such and such a person was to be found; in so small a place the chances were that they would know. The person enquired after might have gone to his piece of land, or down to Sibaris or Corigliano on the coast, or to a neighbouring village. The reply would be the same: '*è andato fuori*' – he has gone outside. Outside – a poetic statement of a clear sense of place. He had stepped beyond the emotional structure of the village and was therefore in truth 'outside'. *Fuori* was a place where a person met forces beyond the reach of the *paese*, or for that matter beyond its understanding, a demonic world that began the moment he was lost to view between two fragments of time – lost to existence as S. Giorgio Albanese understood it.

I wrote a book about those S. Giorgio days, *The Net and the Quest* – the Net being the pattern of relationships the community relies upon, the Quest being the identity those relationships demand. I went back three years later with a BBC team to make a film, *S. Giorgio's Bitter Fruits*, based on that book.

In that interval of three years the changes I had sensed in progress in my earlier stay had become clearer. Some S. Giorgesi recoiled from the words 'bitter fruits' in the film's title, though they referred to forces of which they themselves had often spoken.

In *The Net and the Quest* I illustrated the enclosed, private horizon of the culture with an anecdote about 'another English *professore*' who had passed through the village 'not so long ago'. I was curious about this intruder in what I had come to think of as *my* discovery. Careful probing revealed that the Englishman was Norman Douglas, who had passed through the district, though seemingly not S. Giorgio itself, sixty-four years earlier – a visit mentioned in

Old Calabria (1915). They had dredged up a piece of folk-memory, and compressed time and shifted place in the process.

When writing *The Net and the Quest* I had not read his later book, *Looking Back*, published in 1933, where he mentions a later visit to the region in 1931, to the College at S. Demetrio Corone, of special antiquarian interest to him, but gives no hint of having visited any other Italo-Albanese village. Even if whispers of that later visit had filtered through the remote ravines into the common memory, it was still a considerable time, forty-four years, before my arrival in S. Giorgio.

In outlook and tradition, not much had changed since Norman Douglas's early meanderings in the province. In *Old Calabria* he makes a puzzling comment on the use of English in the Italo-Albanian villages: 'numbers of the men . . . express themselves correctly in English, which they pick up in the United States.'

In my innumerable discussions in S. Giorgio no memory emerged – not even legend – of migrants having returned from America to resume permanent residence in their *paese* of origin. In the distant past a few had returned on brief visits but these had ceased long before. In the places Norman Douglas says he did visit – S. Cosmo Albanese, Vaccarizzo Albanese and S. Demetrio Corone – his presence may have coincided with that of visiting migrants, and in a polite gesture they were presented to him.

In my conversations each day, in the piazza, in people's homes, on mule tracks and pathways in the *campagna*, in the bar where the only public telephone was – for most people the only means of contact with sons or husbands working in the north of Italy, in Germany and Switzerland, making it a place of many comings and goings – I found only one echo of English in S. Giorgio, a curious one, for it was an isolated instance of migration in reverse. People said I must talk to the *Americana*, a woman who had come from America long ago to be the wife of a local man. One of the priests arranged for me to visit her. She was a reserved woman in her late fifties or early sixties, a

widow, enveloped in a flowered wrap-round apron. I imagined her
journeying across the world alone as a very young woman, des-
patched from America like a parcel, to settle in S. Giorgio. She strove
to recover a few words of English. Slowly, with a tremor of sadness,
a few words came. With a shy smile on her bony features she showed
me a little gold ring on her finger, her graduation ring from her
school in America. She had not spoken a word of English since she
had arrived here in her teens. She knew of no one in any of the
nearby Italo-Albanese *paese* who spoke English. She said: 'I would
have known if there was anyone in all the years. I would have kept
the English if I could have.' Her eyes moistened.

'Do you write to your family in America?'

She tugged at the cord of the shapeless apron: 'There is no family.
And I have lost the writing. I knew it good at school.'

She looked past me to the window and the vista of mountains
shaded with terraces, eyes large and clear now, and reverted to
Italian, heavily slurred. She said: 'All is lost. My sons have gone. I
wait.'

That meeting summed up the accumulated sadness of transition
– where nothing ever matched any ideal, and no adjustment was
trivial.

In the three years between my original sojourn in S. Giorgio and
my return with the film crew, something shattering had happened
to the community: drugs had appeared – or, more precisely, had
come to the surface. The awakening must have been made more
painful by the presence of the BBC camera crew, perceived as
taking away on film an irredeemable impression of the community.
Since it was I who had brought the BBC to S. Giorgio, their
relationship with me was being reassessed – and I wondered how
much of the old confidence, slowly built up, was now tinctured
with reserve. In the months of my earlier stay the flow of talk and
sensibility had been warm, though naturally cautious at first. But
now, with the camera's unwinking eye upon them in piazza and

narrow street and church and on the *campagna*, that trust was being re-examined.

In the film unit's ten-day stay, I lodged in a house above the church at the northern entrance to the village, and went down a steep path each morning to breakfast in a bar newly opened by one of the few men who had returned from working in the north to live in the village again. The bar was on the edge of the village proper, on a bypass road recently completed to enable trucks in particular to avoid the tortuous final ascent to the village and the narrow thoroughfare through it on their way to settlements deep in the Sila. The little house, its ground floor given over to the bar and a few tables, and a back room for winter use, was perched on the edge of the ravine that separated S. Giorgio from another village, Vaccarizzo Albanese.

Those July mornings in the pure mountain air were uplifting, the sun drawing gleams of slaty blue, green, yellow from crags capped with clear blue sky. I sat at a table beside the road facing the lofty cliff with S. Giorgio on its crown that overhung the new road swinging round its base. The ravine was dry, its steep sides a blazing green with myriad dots of sunlight diamond bright on spear-like blades of grass. On the further lip of the ravine the grey houses of Vaccarizzo slept. On my first morning all seemed peaceful, untroubled.

While I sat waiting for my breakfast coffee and rolls, a woman neighbour from my previous stay stopped at my table: 'Do you see *that*?' She pointed to a young woman passing by. I recognised her from my discussion groups in the church, but she was much changed from the healthy country girl I remembered – now pale as paper, and very thin. The woman continued: 'Can you believe what happened two days ago? This —' she suppressed the epithet, spluttering in fury. 'This "*nice girl*" lay in the road, white as death. Drugs! It is fortunate to be on its feet now. Fortunate the ambulance came up quickly from the *pianura* to get it to hospital. Look at it! It was a nice girl when you were here. Now? What are we to do?' She roughly wiped her hands on her apron as if her words had soiled them: 'The evil comes from the big cities in *Alt'Italia*. Things we never knew before. The people say the television brings it. What is to become of us?'

It was hard to find the right words.

The crew filmed a baptism in the church. It was conducted by a young priest who had come to the village in the three years I had been away. The two incumbents of my time, men of a certain age, had gone; they had been criticised for being 'too strict'. When I visited Signora Michelina, whose house had been my home three years before, she would not put the criticism into words, but it was easy to guess. I remembered one occasion in particular, when one of the priests had spoken of the *paese* with special sadness: 'The Church has become powerless to maintain moral discipline, or even moral thinking. Marriage, baptism, funeral, there is not much of substance left. People cling to relics of – yes, of superstition.'

'In case they turn out to be wrong?'

He had lifted his thin face and thought about it. 'I see what you mean. In case their materialism, their egotism, turn out disappointingly, they maintain a foothold in the Church? It is not a pleasant thought.'

Sincere, honourable men, they may have spoken out too strongly against the acquisitive restlessness, the urge to abandon a culture suddenly perceived as too limited, too restrictive, which had mysteriously lost its former ability to hold the structure steady – the classic circular 'complaint' of people turning away from a culture because of weaknesses in it which they themselves had helped to create.

The young priest complained stoically that of the many young people who left the *paese* to work in the north few were expected to return. An even smaller number who from lingering sentiment or yielding to parental entreaty came back to get married in the church

– and fewer still for a baptism – went away with no sign of wanting to return. The life of the village, formerly accepted without question, was no longer enough. The one to be found in faraway Turin or, further still, in Germany, was by comparison rich, independent, free of outworn claims. That it was emotionally etiolated by exile was sometimes unwillingly acknowledged, but shrugged away.

He might have been echoing sentiments that had surfaced in my discussion groups when I was there before, described in *The Net and the Quest*. When I had asked the youngsters – then mostly under twenty – if they would remain in the *paese* if the life of S. Giorgio changed to resemble what they imagined obtained in Turin or Milan, there had been a shamefaced hesitancy, the guilt of children who flout authority while obscurely uneasy about the success of their defiance.

Girls of about seventeen had talked of the need to find a new *ambiente* in order to 'realise oneself' – which for some unstated reason was not possible in S. Giorgio. Others had nodded agreement. No one knew what self-realisation meant. The idea might have come at random from some filtering through of distant 'hippy' word-spinning. Did they really think, I had asked gently, that no one had ever 'realised' themselves in the *paese*? There had been silence. Evidently none wanted to consider that possibility.

In older groups, ranging from the twenties to middle-age, there had been greater awareness and greater perplexity. A man of about thirty said: 'We lived ten in the house. The pigs kept it warm in winter. We had enough to eat. We were together and that was good enough. Why has it stopped being good enough? The old people will die and the *paese* will be moribund and there will be nothing left of the things we knew. What has happened to us? How can we save what is left?'

When the film was shown in Britain some people thought my questioning of the ends and means of living was unfair. What was wrong with the desire for 'betterment', worthy ambition of the early social reformers? How could I of all people, formed in the poverty of the Gorbals, argue in favour of deprivation under the dubious banner of holism? Deprivation, I replied, was unqualified only at starvation level, as I knew from experience. The Gorbals had also taught me that you needed the things of the heart as well as bread. Any 'want' above that level was a matter of choice, of comparison, of desired identity. Unfortunately it was an easier decision to pursue the material, where 'rewards' were unmistakeable, than the spiritual, where doubt was part of the given. People often pretended that the spiritual could be dispensed with, but in reality they were in flight from the self-enquiry it demanded.

In one of the film's closing scenes a group senior girls from the church high school, the *magistrale*, their schooldays ending, cluster at the rail at the edge of the 'windowsill' in front of the church, and argue excitedly with Sister Gabriella for the importance of realising themselves by leaving the *paese*. I stand a little apart, elbows on the rail, looking at the flat land far below, while their voices tumble and sparkle like fountains in the sunlight – and Gabriella, near enough in age to understand their hunger for flight, talks of the eternal verities of home. I turn and move along the rail, separating myself from them, and say to myself: 'They *will* go. They will all go. But one day in the future, one or more of them will return – as Peer Gynt returned to *his* home from his wanderings across the world – and say, with him: "Fool that I was! My empire was *here*."'

Being a witness on this fateful threshold of theirs brought questions to myself. Was it arrogance to believe that any interference could save them?

A print of the film was sent to the *sindaco* – the mayor – of S. Giorgio for the people to see. I learnt that they had viewed it 'calmly'. I gathered that the bitter fruits of the title were not denied – an open verdict.

It would be no comfort to them to know, if anyone ever cared to tell them, that for S. Giorgio and a few communities like it, history had delayed the decay that had overtaken countless others in Europe several generations before.

The nineteenth century had tried to convince itself that everyone would prosper from development, that the consequent disruptive social change – to the extent that it was foreseen – would not be as damaging as it turned out to be. Or that 'losses' would be outweighed by gains, as the *magistrale* girls argued, unaware that they were not comparing like with like. However, by no means everyone did prosper. Many did not believe that what was on offer was worth the social and personal cost. William Barnes (1801–86), the Dorset poet, wrote of the breaking strain in his own day with deep seriousness, aware that his cause was lost:

> *Let other folk make money faster,*
> *In the dark-roomed air of towns;*
> . . . .
> . . . .
> *. . . for me, the apple tree,*
> *Do lean down low, in Linden Lea.*

How far had I ever compared the life of S. Giorgio with that of the 'backward' Gorbals? It had not seemed to me at the time that I had done so at all. I saw that I must have done it unawares, if only to convince myself of my good faith in going to live there, that I was contributing something of myself in doing so. Of course no exact comparison with the Gorbals could be made in physical or social detail but one *was* valid enough emotionally. Suggestions that I had acquired a middle-class outlook and a consequent lack of realism on my long journey from the Gorbals, and therefore looked at the life of S. Giorgio with cloudy romanticism, were too facile. The facts were plain. If there was the slightest possibility that further decay could be delayed or made less damaging – as history and chance had done for the *paese* in the past – surely the attempt would be worth while?

Certainly my time in S. Giorgio had had a significant effect in reverse: it had made me examine the Gorbals influence afresh. The Gorbals world picture lived within me more firmly than I had ever thought it could at this distance – insistent on knowing reality even if the knowledge was painful.

In the intervals between filming sessions, seeing myself and my earlier time in the *paese* with unaccustomed detachment, I often recalled the bizarre antiphonies of my first few months in the village, when the locals tried to determine my true purpose in coming among them, reluctant to believe that anyone would do so from benevolent curiosity alone. I wondered if Norman Douglas had met the same suspicions.

Some had thought I was a CIA agent, others that I was a spy for the Italian government. Was it likely that a man from Glasgow would be sent from Rome for such a purpose? However, they only had my word for where I came from.

In time they must have concluded that I was an unfathomable eccentric who, equally mystifyingly, was well intentioned. That might also have been their grandfathers' opinion of Norman Douglas.

While they made up their minds, the classic cry of *miseria* was bandied about in my hearing. On a cold mountain evening, the *tramontana* like an icy arrow chilling the air in the piazza straight from distant Monte Pollino, a man patted his belly that bulged under the traditional ankle-length cloak: 'This is how we are, *dottore*, stomach empty, full of *miseria*.'

The word *miseria* was meant to strike a chord. It did, but not the one they intended. They could not know that *miseria* was not a new idea for me – in the Gorbals I had lived with it constantly. I sympathised with them, however, and tried to show it. After all, they had not asked for my presence among them. It was natural for them to appeal to stereotypes about the *Mezzogiorno* that would be recognised in the north in *Alt'Italia*. S. Giorgio had had a communist *sindaco* for many years. The *Mezzogiorno,* as everyone knew, was a deprived region. They played their part.

I sensed that my talks with Padre Eugenio and Padre Demetrio – the priests in the village at that earlier time – and with the nuns at the *magistrale,* brought a lessening of suspicion, and a cautious willingness to join me in looking at the condition of the *paese*; not a dropping of reserve, but a conditional lessening of it.

When the young people went home and talked about my discussion groups at the church, the older generation must have been stirred to a more profound awareness of the cracks in the old culture. Many of the youngsters had already declared their ambition to turn their backs on the *paese*; but the elders must have comforted themselves by assuming that the young folk's absence would be temporary, as it had been for those who had gone before them in their own generation – when men went north to work for a few years and returned, often to buy land with those earnings – and settled in the *paese* fully again. Many parents must have recoiled from the thought that the new generation, this time round, viewed the *paese* differently in this changed epoch and saw it no longer as a natural place in which to re-establish themselves in the future, but as a monument to a life that had been silenced.

I met only two men who had returned for good while relatively young, and another who was not sure – who waited for his soul to 'settle'. They were in their thirties. For them, perhaps not as acquisitive as others, the old emotional influences were stronger – but only just – than the attractions of a 'free', more affluent, but exiled life in the north.

The priests were not heartened by this new awareness – it did not herald a new awakening for S. Giorgio. The older generation had unthinkingly encouraged the latest eagerness to leave by transmitting to the young folk a weakened faith, together with the hunger for the new consumerism in the north – stimulated by television recently beamed into the villages by reflectors built on the heights.

The old agrarian economy could not support that higher level of demand, and the mood of the young people did not suggest any intention of maintaining a stream of remittances from the north.

I could stay on in S. Giorgio for years more and dig deeper. But *where* was I really digging? Not, I now realised, in S. Giorgio alone. That thought was emphasised in apocalyptic fashion the night before I was to depart – the film shot, the reports on the 'rushes' satisfactory. My ties with S. Giorgio would remain within me wherever I went, but I needed to go, and quickly.

The night was hot and still, the sky a velvet dark blue, the air pressed down with the almost palpable heaviness one senses before a storm. At about three in the morning I was wakened by the door being rattled violently as by a powerful hand trying to force it open – strange, for it was not locked. I sat up in wonder. Could I have dreamt it? No. The door *had* shaken in its frame. The vibrations still hung in the air. Yet the curtains at the open window were still. From somewhere in the house came faint sounds of people moving about. I got out of bed and opened the door. The stone staircase was empty and no further sound came. I went to my window, which looked out on an alley at the back of the house that ran beside the ruined village wall. From the direction of the piazza, voices sounded. Late travellers perhaps, though that was unusual. I stood there for some minutes, with the eerie feeling that whatever had happened was in some fashion connected with my departure – to mark a break with something in myself not yet identified, a fixed position that had served its unknown purpose. What *was* it telling me – and when would I know enough to act upon it?

The air seemed hotter than before. The beginnings of a thought floated away before I could grasp it. I would look for an answer in the morning. I went back to bed and slept.

Next morning the air had lost some of the oppressive weight of the night but there was still the feeling of a brooding presence. On my way down to the bar for breakfast, on the steep alley behind the church, I was greeted by a woman coming out of the bakery, whose house was a few doors away. In an anxious tone she said: 'Why were you not in the piazza in the night – are you all right?'

'Why in the night?'

'The *terremoto*! The house shook! How could you not know? People go to the piazza quickly, even in their nightclothes, when that happens! You never know, you see?'

How could I have forgotten that the whole region was an earthquake zone! I said: 'The door of my room shook violently – but I have never been in an earth tremor before, so I did not think of it. Strange that no one in the house woke me.'

She stared for a fraction of a second and seemed to consider her next words carefully: 'Perhaps they forgot you were there?' She turned quickly and went on her way.

Yes, it *was* time to go. I had delved perhaps deeper than I had realised. I felt the delayed shiver that sometimes comes when a danger has passed, leaving a listening silence within.

The evening before, I had dined with the BBC team at a trattoria down on the coast not far from their hotel in Rossano – convenient for *them*, but not for me; for it meant that after dinner I had to drive nearly twenty miles back up the mountain to S. Giorgio. But I had chosen to lodge in S. Giorgio during the filming as a mark of loyalty to the *paese*.

The solitary drive along the coast and up the mountain after midnight seemed to draw a fitting line under the S. Giorgio experience – but not the emotional depth of it, whose significance I was sure would never fade. The Ionian coast road curved away to the north, where distant groups of lights marked its course against the dark velvet sky, Schiavonea, Sibari, Trebisacce . . . and far beyond, a faint gleam in the sky hinted at the great sprawl of Taranto behind the horizon.

I stopped at the little gap on the left where a hand-painted finger-post pointed upwards to the black bulk of the mountain, a shade darker than the sky, where S. Giorgio Albanese slept on its ledge. I turned the wheel and drove into the narrow side road and stopped. Was this the last time I would climb this road? I wanted to mark the moment. I got out and stood for some minutes trying to reach out to the genius of the place, the empty, secretive road, the fields and trees that clasped to themselves their old, guarded life. I reminded myself that on those dark heights where S. Giorgio and the nearby Albanese settlements were hidden, I had found ancient ritual still observed, whose origins no one knew, that brought to mind primordial practices described by the anthropologist James Frazer in *The Golden Bough*. I paced quietly round the car as if I beat the bounds of my understanding, rendered homage to the spirit of S. Giorgio and to all that it had taught *me*.

Was this really my last time here? Who could say never? I got into the car and drove on up the road, which climbed slowly, bending and twisting, thrusting between small fields and plantations, a dark world holding itself separate. How many times had I done this climb? So many that they were joined together in a journey that had no beginning and could have no end.

In the still, hot night air the delicate scent of cactus fruit floated into the car, a perfume that had greeted me on my first ascent of this road four years before, which would always return to mark the crossing of a frontier.

Isolated houses stood well back from the road, many with a three-wheeler pick-up truck – almost an identification symbol for the *Mezzogiorno* – parked at the side. A few houses near the road had windows boarded up, long abandoned. Far above on the heights no lights showed; the ledge on which S. Giorgio stood jutted out below it, blocking the view of it from below, doubtless a factor determining the original strategic positioning of the fortified village. No other lights showed. The raucous note of the little Fiat in low gear battered the night – and the darkness and the silence tried to shut it out.

At last, as I negotiated yet another hairpin bend in the road, a little line of lights appeared on the heights. I imagined badgers peering out warily at the world. Those lights had every right to be defensive. They prompted a strange thought, a warning that this last climb of mine to S. Giorgio *was* one too many. The village deserved to live in peace. I ought to turn the car in the road and drive away at once. Never mind my luggage ready packed. For I myself felt many questions clamouring for answers within me, more than I had suspected – just as the S. Giorgesi must feel. Obduracy, disguised as common sense, made me dismiss the warning.

It returned reinforced next morning when I thought of the *terremoto* in the night, whose pressures must have been gathering in power even as I drove up the secretive road.

The earth tremor had done no damage. Later it occurred to me that it might have been part of the preparation for the destructive earthquake some months later in the Salerno region. At the first news of it, when it was not yet clear from news reports how far south the effects had been felt, I telephoned the *sindaco* from London to ask if all was well in S. Giorgio. A little surprised, he said all was quiet. 'Not much happens here.'

Some years before, living in Positano, we had been wakened in the middle of the night by a mighty storm that battered the ears, rattled windows and doors, brought huge waves climbing the gothic crags. Its fury had a deliberate quality. Next morning a *carabinieri* loudspeaker van toured the area to announce that there had been an earthquake in Sicily and warn of unseasonable high tides. That storm, too, had come when we were preparing to move on. It was easy to feel, as the ancients must have done in the face of cataclysmic events, that the earth's turnings were intended to remind one of mortality, warn against sloth and delay, against turning away from questions deeply hidden – stir the instincts of propitiation, of sympathetic magic. The terrible thunder and lightning, the savage wind, were summoned by the demons within to demand new visions, new departures. What new voices should we turn to, what old ones turn away from? What was finished? What should be started?

In the Positano days, long before the idea of writing *Growing up in the Gorbals* was even a mirage in the distance of the mind, Jacqueline had urged me to write about the Gorbals life. Why had I resisted so strongly? It might have been modesty, but as I questioned myself again and again, that reason became trivial, almost irrelevant – there was too much emotion invested in the past. Looking back I think I feared to resurrect unmanageable visions of childhood and youth, almost certainly not comprehended at the time, which later I elegiacally recalled and misunderstood all over again, when it was too late for 'solutions'. How could I envisage solutions now, and to what end? That too was not a good enough reason. It took me some time to see that it was the Gorbals itself that challenged me to turn and face it down.

I saw that nearly everything I had written before, however passionately I had campaigned, had been detached – though not consciously. The demons had kept certain doors locked – which must be the doors I was now being urged to open. That last night in S. Giorgio, when the door had mysteriously rattled and wakened me, and I had gone to the window to look for a cause and found that all was quiet without – I must have been prompted, more powerfully than before, to search within and try to fathom where I really stood, and why the need to turn away and face the Gorbals had risen again so strongly. Before I knew that I had just lived through an earthquake, the thought that after all I *would* write about the Gorbals must have taken hold at last; and there could be no further debate within. I saw that I *needed* to write it, and there was no escape.

It would be four years before I started writing the book and challenged the Gorbals chimera, revived old shadows and fears. As I tried to see their meaning clearly enough to set it down, their menace returned – so much so that in my new-born sense of urgency mixed with doubt, areas of darkness obstinately remained.

Now, thirteen years after starting to write *Growing up in the Gorbals*, as I recall again the scene in the film when the *magistrale* girls proclaimed to Sister Gabriella the rightness of their hunger to depart, some Gorbals perplexities return and demand to be looked at afresh; and I understand why I am driven to communicate yet again with my juvenile experience, as I imagine those girls communicating with theirs one day in the future, in fuller self-examination.

'*I call to remembrance my song in the night; I commune with mine own heart; and my spirit made diligent search.*' [Psalms 77:6]

EIGHT

The Esther Labyrinth

I THOUGHT OF WERNER, RIGOROUS THINKER THAT HE WAS, WHO had always seemed immune from doubt, and his struggle with himself to recover control after his wife and children were killed in a German bomber raid soon after landing in England to join him. He blamed himself for remaining in England instead of going with them to America in the first place. He said one day apropos of nothing: 'It does not matter what recalls us to faith, only that we make the attempt!'

Seeing me nonplussed, he went on quickly: 'Yes – I am not a paragon of religious observance. *You* know that. But faith is necessary. The part of me that is a scientist knows that too. Above all things, faith means knowing *what* we are first of all, but there is a devil inside that makes us turn away from that perception. He entices us to try on many masks, knowing none will fit, that they are transitory experiments, making us waste time and dream of failure.'

The startling confession stirred me to offer some self-examination of my own. It was probably nearer the surface than I suspected.

In childhood I had experimented with responses to the world, as if picking bits of costume for a school play out of the class dressing-up box, or dreamlike visions of masks to fit Will o' the Wisp images of who I was. The dreams persisted long after – and not only dreams but experiments with identity. Was that what Werner had meant by 'knowing what we are'? The occasional gleam of light, often too fleeting to be understood? A riddle from long ago came to mind: 'How can one be faithful to an unknown purpose?'

And lines of James Elroy Flecker spoke within:

> *White on a throne or guarded in a cave*
> *There lies a prophet who can understand*
> *Why men were born . . .*

Some of those masked versions of myself returned again and again, reminders of reaching out to new experience, blindly as it often seemed in retrospect – and of the responses, still articulate in the long gallery of memory. Returning ghosts questioned me.

What was it I had tried so hard to convey, they asked, when it was perfectly clear what I was? I had been trying – as Werner did – to assuage a recurring emptiness of the spirit that threatened to destroy the will. Even so, the temporary confidence each mask brought supported my search for the ideal object of love, to grasp and hold for ever. Each mask was the best picture of myself I could conjure, though it was never the golden image glimpsed in child-hood and pursued ever after – as Hoffman pursued *his* real image, doomed never to hold it steady long enough to possess it.

The relationship with Esther was a volcanic experience whose significance remained powerful, perhaps because she responded, in that spark of time, to my attempt to create a bridge between the worlds of Oxford and the Gorbals. I did not know that that was my purpose till long after.

There were other false moves, none quite as wounding, but wounding enough, in Oxford encounters, with girls of bewildering sophistication and correctness – or so they struck me till I began to understand something of Oxford's codes, and found that these girls were not as correct as I had thought; in a punt in the shade of a weeping willow or in a hollow in Wytham Woods, and one in particular who liked to invoke, in an arch prelude, 'the laws of the Medes and Persians which altereth not'!

Esther had gleaming brown hair down to the middle of her back, creamy features with a dizzying quality of light and innocence and eagerness. I met her during a vacation visit to Glasgow in my first Oxford year when I had begun to see that I was still in shock from the transition to Oxford, and that the Gorbals I saw was indefinably different from the one I had known so short a time before.

She was from a 'respectable' family, which in Gorbals parlance referred to economic status, people reaching up towards the lower-middle class – superior craftsmen such as tailor's cutters, or small businessmen. Strictly speaking, her family were not of the Gorbals proper but lived a short distance south of the Gorbals border, off Pollokshaws Road.

I first saw her in the street, as I thought by chance, as I stood at the open door of Uncle Zalman's clothes repair shop. Aunt Rachel had asked me to be there at a particular time to do an errand for my uncle, but when I arrived punctually he was finishing an urgent job, and told me to stand at the open door. They wanted me to be seen by the whole world, they told me in pride – *their* Oxford nephew! That knowledge was uncomfortable. What vision of theirs did they expect me to fulfil?

A lovely girl halted on the littered pavement just outside the shop door, hesitated, looked past me into the shop, swung on her heel in a half-turn and back again as if making sure of her direction, again looked at me and at the inside of the shop, and with a toss of her head stepped away with click-clack of heels towards Pollokshaws Road. All the busy noise of the world, the street cries, horses stamping and snorting between cart shafts, hum of tramcars, was silenced. I wanted to follow the goddess, forget all else. I had lacked the courage to step out on to the pavement and speak to her while she hesitated. I had forgotten all the opening gambits I had ever heard of. I was humbled. I followed her erect back till she disappeared in the distance where Cumberland Street railway bridge crossed over. I turned away from the door into the room filled with hissing steam and the banging of Uncle Zalman's press-iron. All else was the same, but I was changed for ever. How was I to live, now that I had seen her?

Aunt Rachel had been watching through a tiny gap in the curtains draped across the glass panel of the door at the back of the shop, behind which was their combined living-room, kitchen and bedroom. She beckoned me in, her lined face shining in gladness: 'I saw and I am pleased for you – but it is early yet! From that look she gave you I can see she likes you. And you? I can see it in your face. I knew she was going to pass when you would be standing there! That was important, you see. She is a good girl. Her name is Esther. Leave it to me.'

I was slow to grasp what she meant by 'I knew she was going to pass . . .' Two contrary visions fought within me. I did not know that I was trying to see the Gorbals from two perspectives at once, that of mannered Oxford, and the old, wary one of the Gorbals, and was blinded by the contrast: old visions no longer clear, new ones blurring the old hard outlines, as when one tries to see through the wrong spectacles. The Oxford lenses were too new to depend upon; the Gorbals insisted on being judged by its own rigid canons alone. I was lost between the two.

My aunt arranged for me to meet Esther at her parents' home as protocol demanded. Social life in the 'respectable' milieu was grounded on conventions designed to protect a girl's good name, as well as guard against mixing too freely – if at all – at lower-income levels. Mixing 'up' was approved of – mixing 'down' was not. Being in business, rather than working for wages, earned some relaxation of the rules. Uncle Zalman's clothes repair shop, not much bigger than a large packing case, was undeniably a business, and gave him and Aunt Rachel a footing in that milieu, where my aunt could advance family interests in the marriage market beyond the Gorbals.

When she told me the introduction was arranged, I sensed a certain hardness behind the warmth, scars of suffering, of old disappointments: 'My child, you must look to your future. That is a fine respectable girl and you must put other thoughts out of your mind. Be a gentleman with her. Learn about her slowly. I speak to you as my poor sister your mother, may she rest in peace, would have spoken if she had been spared to see you *now*, in your days of success.'

Things moved quickly. Esther spoke little at our first meeting in her parents' presence. Her father, a short, compact man with a keenly appraising air, set out the conditions for 'walking out' with her – where we were permitted to go and for how long, as if setting out the conditions for doing business with a potential supplier – still to be fulfilled. He hinted unmistakably at what was prohibited – with nods from his wife as if she monitored his words from a script. She clicked her teeth now and then, partly to emphasise the warnings, partly in impatience. Esther seemed to share her mother's mood, a blend of pursuit and prudence – balanced in favour of pursuit, at least for the moment. That I was at Oxford seemed to dazzle both mother and daughter as if I was El Dorado himself. I wondered what the mother would think if she knew how little money I had in my pocket – a carefully measured portion of my scholarship money, with nothing to spare for luxuries.

These thoughts must have prompted me to make a rash choice for our first evening out together. I took her to a restaurant near Sauchiehall Street whose sign swinging above the street door, a picture of a bewigged cavalier, had stirred boyhood fancies long ago. I had passed it countless times on my way to and from the Mitchell Library and, seeing expensively dressed people go through its doors, dreamed that one day I would be numbered among them. I knew I was mad to pretend I could afford it, but that thought alone – risking all for love – went to my head.

As for Esther, like most office girls she took sandwiches to eat in her lunch hour, and could have had little or no experience of 'eating out'. The Cavalier must have struck her as high living whose like she had glimpsed only at the cinema.

I was borne up on visions of magic and romance. I ordered a bottle of wine and tried not to be rattled by the surprise on the white-haired waiter's face – I had forgotten to look at the menu. He must see through my paper-thin attempt at sophistication, in my Burton's houndstooth tweed jacket and crumpled grey flannel bags, khaki shirt and red tie.

Esther, in a dress of fine navy-blue wool that clung and curved and tantalised, bewitched me. Attentive, careful of her deportment, somewhat awed by the surroundings, she applied herself to fit my mood and the occasion. How brilliantly she shone, how perfect she was.

Couples came in, men in well-tailored suits, some with double-breasted waistcoats, women with fox furs on one shoulder and draped down from the other. The head waiter greeted some of them by name. Would I ever belong to that favoured company? As they passed our table near the frosted-glass windows, they gave no sign that they saw me as an interloper in their world, or saw me at all. I was uncomfortably aware that my proletarian khaki shirt and aggressive cloth tie were out of place among starched white collars and silk ties and gold cuff-links. Then I remembered the many Oxford students who proclaimed in raffish dress the rebellious zeitgeist. If that was good enough for those members of the boss class, these habitués of The Cavalier might mistake me for one of their own after all. Did I want to pass for one of the boss class? That was a poser. Evidently I did! Was it Esther and her 'respectable' status that wooed me away from the old cause? Who was I betraying now? Where was the torch of redemption that Bernard's dying father had given me to carry onwards for him? And Mr Wolf and the whole company of the Workers' Circle?

Would Esther forgive my aping the boss class? If she was aware of it at all, coming from that family, she might even applaud it as a sign of wholesome ambition.

The ambience of lustrous mahogany, deep red carpet, rose-tinted lighting, attentive service, lifted me up. Was I trying to show her the person I would become, who would one day command all this as of right?

I sensed an answering gleam in her, the creamy features infused with red. A different uncertainty brought me down to earth. What did I want from this enactment with her? How was I to achieve it? No, that was the wrong way to be thinking of it. It should simply *happen* – as it had with Annie, spontaneous combustion of delight from one moment to the next! Aunt Rachel's words returned: 'Be a gentleman with her' – which must mean the opposite.

She had also said: 'Get to know her slowly.' On that view, between this correct dinner table to the achievement of desire was a very long distance, unimaginably painful. Sitting here with me was the treasure house of delight. Was she willing me to unlock it? Voices clamoured in my head, what to do, how to say it – was it all happening too quickly? No, I must not betray lust too soon, or too crudely, lest I spoil everything.

Visions of Annie intruded, of dreamlike delight in what seemed a remote past, though it was so near. Her nakedness pressed against me in the bracken as she took up the piece of flint to scratch on a remnant of Roman masonry the date of her transition from one state of the flesh to another.

Oxford had taught me in these few months, already a lifetime, that the world had no patience with innocence – that I must learn a minuet of intuition, prudence, correctness. Yet Esther seemed to be telling me that this was no time for the leisured pace. I needed to divine what to do, and waste no time.

Her expression had changed. That look asked a question as plainly as if she had spoken it: the evening was passing, and what did I want of her?

To postpone words I reached for the bottle to fill her glass, but the waiter anticipated me with ceremonial panache, then knowingly retreated. I raised my glass to her. A newly discovered sensibility was at last making the bridge I wanted. I was reaching out for certainty at any price. Yes I *was* sure. She blushed again as if I had spoken, though I had said nothing. A whisper came to me, confusing me again, telling me to discard the primitive Gorbals way with women, exemplified in Alec's words, where courtship meant no more than manoeuvre for conquest. My demon wanted me to say something altogether different, but the words were still out of reach.

I wanted to win her from a heart that was full, in a way that was beyond any doubt. The meal must not end with us no further forward. I talked and talked, waiting for the demon to tell me what to do.

She sipped the heavy wine and searched my face. In those steady eyes a shadow was forming. Could I hold time in suspense till I found the new language? Then I saw that a different fear prevented me; I did know what to say, but feared I would be betrayed again.

I remembered that Alec, from his years of seniority, had seen Annie's betrayal, and her subsequent attempt to entrap me into marriage, as acts of desperation, confronting life in the only way she knew. She was to be pitied, if not forgiven. After all, I had taken what she had to give when it suited me. Life unwound with awesome fixity. He had spoken with his customary laconic roughness, with the *ennui* of seeing nothing new in the world.

I had gone to meet him the previous evening at the factory in Stockwell Street. The hands had been doing overtime, turning out samples for the autumn trade though it was still spring. I had the eerie feeling that I saw the past imprints of my feet on the stairs rising steeply behind the street door, never to be erased. Men's boots thumped down, filling the stone staircase with thunder, then marched out into the street crowded with home-going workers. Women and girls clacked down after them, ankles tilting on worn heels, and quickly away. Two of them sucked bleeding fingers, the usual wounds from broken sewing-machine needles. A few of the younger ones looked me over in mild curiosity and exchanged glances as if saying: 'That's him back again – remember Annie?'

Alec leaned his spare frame against the brick door frame, an ageless figure, contemplating them as they joined workers from other factories in a ragged column streaming along the rubbish-strewn pavement towards the Clyde bridge and the Gorbals on the far side. His knobbly face cracked in a patient smile. He nodded towards the women and girls streaming away in little groups and giving the men a wide berth. 'They doan' talk aboo' ye an' Annie any mair – it's auld stuff a'ready!'

He slid an open paper packet of five Woodbines from a jacket pocket and in one smooth manoeuvre shook a cigarette to his lips and sparked a match to flame with his thumbnail and lit it, and drew deeply: 'Aye, jist ye look a' them hairies steppin' along with their noses in the air, wantin' ye tae think they're stuck-up respectable yins! An' under them skirts they're nae be'er than us! Ye jist tell 'em the tale wi' a wee bi' o' *guile*! That's a' ye need! An' whi' else is thur?'

Did he guess that I was about to begin walking out with one of the 'stuck-up respectable yins'?

From the floor above came sounds of doors being slammed and the turning of heavy keys in locks. The boss was preparing to go home. 'Come on,' Alec said, 'will we go tae McGinty's and then maybe a game o' billiards?'

McGinty's fish-and-chip shop was in the Saltmarket, the trading quarter dedicated by day to general merchandise, with miscellaneous offices on upper floors – including Bernard's trade union –

and by night to women. For me to see the Saltmarket again, Alec may have thought, would be a salutary corrective to any 'fine ideas' I might have brought with me from Oxford.

Gas streetlamps shone pale gold in the blueish dusk. Street-walkers materialised on fetid pavements, at lamp-post or doorway or broad loading bay, to pirouette and swing with skirts held wide, *their* market open. A throng of men materialised, from offices and market stalls and shops closing for the day, or passing through to confront temptation. The priestesses moved in to take their pick of this first flock.

To their experienced eyes we were not worth the plucking, at least till the hour was late and prime prospects no longer passed through, or trade was slack and prices had to fall.

With swift alchemy the rites began. A priestess touched an arm or hand in instantaneous intimacy, leaned close to reach lower, hips thrusting under tightened skirt. Her intuition accurate, she whisked him into shadowed doorway or dark loading bay. Quite soon afterwards the man reappeared and with sudden swagger strode away, soon followed into the street by his ministrant hurrying into the flock again.

Here was the night world that had drawn me in adolescent fascination – with the attendant fear of the power of woman, repelled by the contrived eagerness, the tragic, calculating faces, willing yet distant. Masks of the Medusa.

Alec said thoughtfully: 'The smells take ye back, eh?'

Vapours from pubs and warehouses and food shops, over-ripe fruit, decaying produce, began to be overlaid by human odours: masculine sweat, drink, intimations of woman stronger and stronger. From the shadows came shufflings and gruff primordial sounds with syncopation of subdued female tones. Some of these dark caverns already gave off the distinctive odour, as of damp starch.

Alec must know that the elemental fury of the place, like the epoch of my life it recalled, was imprinted for ever.

The adolescent fear of woman, the magnetism of the labyrinth between the ivory pillars here cynically offered, did not return in their old strength, but they were powerful still – elegiac resonances of a lost self. I marvelled again at the blind notions of fulfilment here exposed, the interweaving of magic and partial horror. How appropriate that Bernard's office overlooked the arena, where the priestesses Kirstie and Jeanie befriended him.

Life in its partial horror,
Accepted moment by moment . . .

When I had called for Esther earlier that evening, in the heavily furnished parlour darkened by net curtains and long red velvet ones, the rules of 'walking out' were repeated. Again her parents assessed me. Her father measured his words. Her mother, a collected figure in high-necked dark velvet dress, with tight, greying hair and a bun, seemed content to be in her husband's shadow, but only in part. Two conditions were emphasised once more, and she nodded in emphasis. I must bring Esther back by ten-thirty, and I must not take her where we could not be seen.

Being an Oxford student gave me a credit balance to start with, as far as my 'prospects' were concerned – 'all things considered' – a reservation politely but firmly stated; which could only refer to my blighted Gorbals family. Emphatically I was on probation.

Esther had sat next to her father on an upright mahogany chair with a carved back, as she had done on my introductory visit, hands side by side in her lap. She glanced at me guardedly, a gleam of impatience in her eyes.

Aunt Rachel had said that such talk from a girl's parents was to be expected. A respectable girl had to be protected. I must put the old careless life behind me. I thought: 'She knows about Annie!' She added, with bitterness immediately repressed: 'I know what young people can do.' I caught her glance at photographs of her two sons on the mantelpiece, and knew she referred to the neglect with which they had repaid their parents' sacrifice in putting them through university – though I had been too young to understand at the time how wounding their behaviour had been. I thought of what she and Uncle Zalman had done to hold my family together after Mother died and in the face of Father's rages. They were great-hearted people. I resolved to respect her counsel.

Esther's steady radiance swept these thoughts aside. Here was a primitive summons. You accepted all of it or none.

Her very composure raised temptation to white heat. Her challenge was unequivocal, limitless. What could she know about limits at eighteen? She could surely not have tasted anything like the licence I had shared with Annie beside the middens in tenement backyards or in the long grass by the Carbeth track, with no thought of a reckoning?

Her eyes said: 'If I'm not afraid, why should *you* be?' As if by chance her knee touched mine.

Was she playing a game of make-believe with herself and with me, knowing she ran no risk? She knew where I lived, and guessed that I would not dare take her there – apart from anything else, that could not be kept secret, and could ruin her. She must have guessed, too, that I had no money with which to buy secrecy in a hotel. Even if I had, I had no idea where to find one that asked no questions. Was it possible that she knew where to go? She might know more than I thought, if only from gossip among girls in her office.

Years later the enigma of Esther that evening – and my uncertainty in dealing with it – was easier to interpret. For her generation, about three years younger than mine and even more unsettled, the *zeitgeist* had altered. With Armageddon so close, old moralities had weakened still further – and what unassuageable regret they would feel if they permitted a single morsel of fulfilment to escape.

Had I been more mature, I would have been quicker to interpret passing remarks, as when Aunt Rachel had speculated about Esther being 'a bit of a handful' for her parents because of her readiness for danger, even eagerness for it. She had hinted at something else too. Esther's parents, fearing she might soon be too *much* of a handful, might decide on a way of anchoring her that one heard of in Oxford gossip, and read about in novels – get her married off quickly to an otherwise acceptable fellow even if he was poor. His lack of means would make him easier to control. It was not impossible.

High on the wall beside our table, a mahogany pendulum clock struck, and the tremulous brassy tones pierced the hum of talk in the long room – nine o'clock. If only I had planned the evening with greater courage, there could still have been time to take her somewhere private. I could have asked Bernard to get me the address of the shilling room where Kirstie and Jeanie had offered to take us. No, that was unthinkable! How could I take Esther to a prostitute's room?

My head was full of warnings. A different one sounded from afar, from Oxford. If I did find somewhere to take Esther in secret, her parents might come to know of it and denounce me to the authorities in Oxford! One heard of students being disciplined, even expelled. Some made light of it, protected as they were by family and money from serious damage. I had no such cushion.

The sensation of being caught between the pincers of Oxford and Glasgow was almost palpable. Oxford was superficially *louche* but at heart rigid, though one heard of money making it less so. Glasgow people spoke as if old rules of right behaviour were still in command, another sunset vision – sometimes with a smile of derision, as Esther had just spoken of girls she knew who had 'gone further than they should' as if penalties would surely follow, or would they? In the next breath she mocked her parents' view of what was right conduct – yet did so uncertainly; doubt and fear swung in an equal balance. Evidently her parents' fears were well founded.

It is now hard to believe that in those tense late-1930s days of foreboding and futility, people still accepted that life was governed by visions of an age that was past – its assumptions about gallantry, courtesy, generosity of motive, prudent passion, principles of behaviour intrinsically to be valued. Women must not talk to strange men, must observe the 'custody of the eye'. Men must respect and care for women as the weaker sex. A man had a natural duty to protect a woman even from her own 'undesirable' desires – not take advantage of them.

Thus 'walking out' should mean nothing more daring than going to the pictures or a 'Tally shop' – Italian shop – for an ice-cream and a cake, or to the public pathways of the nearest park. Even if you reached the approved stage of going steady there could be no question of passionate experiment. Pretending to uphold those assumptions was important even for many rebels. When the war did come, much of the pretence would melt away.

With Annie there had been no pause between desire and the liberties we took. Nor did we imagine that this behaviour could change the future for us. Only gradually, and too late, did I see that she had drawn ahead of me in maturity, and that her horizons were hidden from me. Her progression to full emotional womanhood, which I must have seen but not understood, had been so subtle that she herself may not have seen it at each stage for what it was. That she acquired an awesome ruthlessness in the process I had refused to believe, presumably because I had no idea how to meet it.

Her spectral presence in The Cavalier reminded me that the border between desire and fulfilment was planted with danger – the life force, which she had conjured in the end. Ever since, I had thought of it as waiting in woman's fleshly vapours for the moment when it must conquer all caution and fulfil its destiny. Now its fumes reached out to me from Esther, as intoxicating as they must have been in Eden. Should I protect her from it? If I did would she understand why and forgive?

I could hear Alec's ironic comment: 'Ye doan' ask yersel' ques-tions like tha'!' In adolescent days his Gorbals sophistication had filled me with awed fascination – as in his rejection of pretence: 'Life hasnae go' a nice face an' ah'm no' goin' tae pretend i' has!'

I wanted to be fully part of that culture – yet at the same time to absorb that other one, which I sensed was richer but in conflict with it, then only attainable through the Mitchell Library and the university evening classes. I did not see that the two world views were already in conflict within me.

Yes, I did want Esther to be respectable no matter what we did together – never mind the contradiction. Our season of walking out must surely take its course before we 'did' anything.

The thought stopped me in my tracks. Vacation had only a week and a half to run, including the four days it would take me to cycle back to Oxford. How was I to fulfil the walking out requirement – of indeterminate length – from four hundred miles away, with no money for the train fare to and fro?

The strawberries and cream arrived. She picked up her spoon but put it down again. Meditatively she turned the thin gold bracelet on her wrist, then ran a forefinger through a curl of hair resting in the curve of her neck. She searched my face. Her question was now insistent: what did I want the next step to be?

I must have panicked then and the wine must have taken over. I talked of a future when she and I would know the other's thoughts through the harmonics of the spirit – a current Oxford conceit. Though the wine spoke, the vision was real. It belonged to the rarefied air on the high peaks; it reached out for a grace of sense and existence beyond day-to-day awareness. It might be granted to no one, or only to a blessed few touched by the Archangel's wing, but there was no escaping the quest. It had to be followed wherever it led.

Her next words showed how wide of the mark I was.

She reddened, hesitated, then said resignedly: 'I've just seen you the way you'll be in the future, when you've got to where you want to be. You're at a big desk in a grand office like in the pictures, and I am sitting there opposite you with my coat on, and the phone rings beside you and you pick it up and say into it: "Hello, my dear, wait a minute." And you look across the desk at me and say: "It's my wife, will you excuse me?" And I get up and leave. That'll be the way you'll be, far above me.'

In prefiguring worldly success for me she was assuming that she could have no part in it. She might even have construed my heady talk as a subtle way of rejecting her.

Desperate to banish the wrong impression – whatever it was – I talked furiously; and again I went to extremes. The future she had 'seen' was the opposite of what I meant. Wherever my new self took me, I wanted her to be at my side. I stopped for breath. How on earth had I got to this point?

Her eyes widened. 'I thought I was not keeping up with you. And now you're saying all these things! I've never met a boy that talked to me like that.'

What great distances had to be travelled? Would I learn in time?

We walked back to Pollokshaws Road, skirting the Gorbals along Eglinton Street, under a clear, steely sky. There was an unfamiliar purity in the air despite the reddish-yellow glare from the plume of flame above Dixon's Blazes. The harsh voice of the Gorbals was muted. We paced the pavement in easy silence.

After a while she murmured: 'Will we walk out for the rest of the time till you go back to Oxford?'

With a twinge of shame I saw I should not have waited for her to ask the question. I said: 'I feel I've been asking you that all evening!' I put my arm about her waist, and she leaned into me and we took each step pressed together as if our flesh was joined.

When we arrived at her close I was reminded of respectability, and turned towards the stairs to go up with her to her house and deliver her to her family as promised. She halted in surprise, then drew me to the rear of the close and into a dark alcove under the stairs, near a rectangular arch that gave on to the back yard, furthest from the gas lamp hanging from an iron bracket on the wall above the lower steps. With quickened breath she said that as we were so near her house – directly under its front door on the floor above – we had 'a good excuse', meaning that we were breaking the code of respectability by an insignificant degree. I wondered if she was making a dire mistake, for I had heard a turbulent rustle in the deep shadow beyond the arch, betraying the presence of another couple in the back yard near the rubbish bins only a few feet away. Her voice may have been recognised.

In our dark cave the world was gone. She led the way in translating dream to reality. When a church clock struck ten-thirty it seemed that only a few seconds had elapsed, but we must have stood entwined for half an hour or more. At the foot of the stairs, where the bubbling gas mantle threw down a cone of yellowish light, she whispered to me to brush away any whitewash that might remain on her clothes from leaning against the wall. She did the same for me. From the back yard beyond the arch, no sound came.

Upstairs, her parents sat stiffly on either side of the tiled fireplace in their parlour, in black horsehair armchairs with white lace draped on back and arms. They looked as though they had been staring at the squat mahogany clock on the mantel shelf.

'Did you have a nice evening, dear?' her mother asked, a tremor in her voice. In addressing the question to Esther she revealed that the putative suitor's views, on this and probably weightier matters, would be of minor interest, if any.

'It was marvellous – *really* marvellous!' Esther cried with shining face, giving me a glance that conjured again the lust of a few minutes before, which now roared through the room like a mill race, so powerful a presence that her parents must surely feel it.

'Yes it *was*,' I said. 'And I am looking forward to others.'

If feminine intuition had its proverbial force, I thought, her mother must have sensed the heat in our veins. I dared not look at Esther, for her colour was high and her whole bearing showed post-pleasure languor and remoteness.

I wondered if we would be denounced by whoever had stood in that shadow beyond the archway at the back of the close. Quite possibly one of that couple, probably the girl, also lived in this close, and knew Esther.

When I called for her on subsequent evenings, her parents were a little friendlier. The couple in the back yard must have had good reason not to make known their own presence there.

We met every evening that week, but I had to watch the pennies, and there could be no more splendour at The Cavalier. We roamed shady spots in Queen's Park till the gates closed at dusk, or sat in the back row of the Plaza cinema in Victoria Road nearby, stopping at a Tally shop to sit at a marble-topped table to eat ice-cream and talk in golden whispers. That quarter being within easy distance of her close, we could home back there earlier than on the first evening, to have more time under the curve of the stairs. We trusted to luck not to be seen approaching the close, her quiet street being ill-lit, with few people about after dark.

Each time, as she led the way into our cave, I dutifully warned: 'What if someone finds us?' — meaning a member of her family. She shook her head and pulled me into the shadows, and the impatient blood shut out everything else.

That I might not be the first to share the enactment with her never occurred to me. She knew far more ways than I had guessed, and certainly more than I myself did, to stir lust even higher, lower the fire to raise it higher still, prolong sensation — demonic alchemy.

When Aunt Rachel had called her a bit of a handful, did she know the full extent of it? Did Esther's parents know? Or guess? Probably they did, which would explain their anxious glances at each other, at Esther, and guardedly at me, each time I brought her back. No wonder Esther impatiently dismissed my sense of responsibility for her when I whispered that I was wrong to take advantage of her — perhaps not entirely seriously, a twinge of guilt, or caution, or even fear. Possessively she pulled me to her: 'Come on!' Her breath was shallow and fast. 'No one's goin' to know! Anyway you're just pretending. Look at you!'

Each night as I walked away among the stars, I conjured her embrace and breathed the warm aroma of her flesh folded against me, life-giving elixir, and offered up a prayer never to be parted from it.

On our last evening under the stairs – I was leaving the next morning to cycle back to Oxford – we swore that our courtship was solid, that we would be faithful to it until we could redeem it for ever at the end of my studies. Nudging her belly even closer she murmured: 'We couldn't be more solid than *this*!'

When I returned at the end of term, I said, I would find a place where we could be really private. I had no idea how; but there must be a way.

'Yes!' she breathed. 'Oh, yes!'

Meanwhile we would keep the courtship going by letter.

She pressed more tightly still: 'I wish we could keep *this* going by letter!'

Upstairs she announced, controlling her breathlessness, that she wanted to continue walking out with me when I came back in eight weeks' time. Her parents smiled to one another across the hearth. Her mother brought me a glass of wine and a piece of ginger cake, not quite a celebration but a seemly gesture to send me on my way.

I wrote to Esther the next day from a youth hostel at the end of the first hundred miles of my ride south. Three days later her reply arrived at college, full of longing and talk of further discoveries we would make together when I came back. We wrote every few days.

Halfway through the term her tone changed; qualification appeared, hints of things she must not commit to paper, seeming to assume that I knew what she meant. I wrote and pleaded to know what had gone wrong. Sleepless nights followed. I got a short reply saying there was 'a lot going on in the family' and she would write fully soon.

A fortnight later, the end of term not many days away, the letter came. Her parents had decided to get her married off quickly. The words 'married off' were underlined. The man chosen was about seventeen years her senior, and had a good business. There were reasons, which must be obvious to me, why she could change nothing. If I was in a position to marry her immediately, things would be different. Between the lines of copperplate I read an unbelievable detachment, gothic in its acceptance of destiny. Was this her parents speaking? Or her own voice? What difference could *that* make! Finally she said she would always love me, but this was her last letter and I must not write again.

A few days later Aunt Rachel wrote unhappily. It would have been such a good match! Why had I not been careful? Why had I let the girl lead me by the nose? The girl must have thought that what she had done put her in a position to dictate to her parents. Women — young or old — could be such fools! Such pathetic fools.

My aunt would not put her meaning any plainer. Did she mean Esther was pregnant? That was impossible. Had Esther invented her 'condition' to make matters go *our* way, and then her parents had turned the tables on her, and used her own story to drive her in another direction altogether?

I tried to telephone her at home. Her mother was polite — almost warm — but firm. Esther, she said, would not speak to me. It would be best if I did not try to communicate with her again.

Among all the hints and guesses, one thing hammered in my head: the irony of fate. If Esther really was pregnant I could not possibly be the cause, for I had refused to let her run that risk. If she was pretending, her only imaginable motive must be the hope of forcing her parents to support her promise to *me*. The more my rattled brain looked at it, the more plausible that was — though there had been no hint of such a scheme in all our talks.

There *was* another possibility, which I tried to dismiss from my mind: there *had* been someone else, and she was not pretending at all.

When would I learn about life, my aunt asked? I should have made doubly sure. It would not have been the first time young people had used the forces of nature to compel a family to consent to a match, and the plan had gone awry.

What did she mean by 'sure'? She must think I *was* responsible! Ah yes, the forces of nature – the life force. Did she know more about Esther than she had told me?

If only I had the money to go to Glasgow at once and take Esther in my arms and elope with her! Ah, no – that was absurd. What would we live on? Obviously the scholarship money would cease; in any case it was only just enough for basic living in term time and vacation even with no extravagance like The Cavalier, to be paid for with belt-tightening afterwards. The alternative, to wait two or more years for my 'prospects' to ripen, which she had seemed to accept, must have become too daunting. Or had her parents decided on peace of mind at any price and opted for an immediate solution? They might even have had the alternative candidate in mind all along!

If I did decamp to Glasgow, what would I be left with? The factory again! Dare I throw away the prize of Oxford? Oh, to stop the world spinning the wrong way!

Yet the facts still nagged at me – what *was* the truth of Esther's story? Reaching that point in my maelstrom of cudgelled brains I began to see that it mattered little what the crude facts were. Where I had thought all was simple, there had been a maze of motive, plan and counter-plan at work, and I had walked blindly into it and lost my way.

My aunt wrote again, in calmer mood, to offer consolation. What had happened was probably for the best – so long as I learned from it. That was the only way to look at *anything* that happened in life. There was no going back along that road and trying to change anything. It was spilt milk. She would look round again for a match for me. But I must learn quickly. Even if a woman meant well, as this girl probably thought she was doing, life could play some bad tricks.

Engulfed though I was in oceanic unhappiness, I saw that she must be hinting at bad tricks life had played on *her*. Thinking of her small, neat figure, much the same height and build as Mother as I remembered her, I marvelled at the courage of them both. I saw that Mother's death had been an escape from the battle, contrived by apocalyptic forces within her. Aunt Rachel, tougher, or luckier, had never stopped fighting. I wondered if this experience was propelling me forward in maturity, as my aunt hinted it might. This was the first time she had allowed her pain to spill out. Why, she asked, did people make the same bad judgements again and again?

She did not say in so many words that I had disappointed her and given her pain, but that was plain. I needed someone to set out for me the mistakes I had repeated. In what ways must I change? Where could I look for guidance? Not to Father, trammelled in his sense of doom; if he had felt confident enough to advise me, he would have done it before. Or perhaps he had, in his laconic fashion, and the substance of it had passed me by? I asked my aunt to tell me the changes I needed to make. She said she could not 'take life to pieces' for me in a letter, and perhaps not at all, for it called for so much heart-searching, so much pain. Perhaps, I asked myself, Father had felt as she did, caught in the toils of futility, and had given up hope. After all, he must have known about Annie, and had said nothing. Aunt Rachel said she had tried to give guidance in her own family — meaning her two sons — and where had it got her? Yes, she would try to find the strength to advise me for her poor sister's sake, but I must be patient. To begin with, here was a lesson for the time being: 'Make up your mind *steadily*, not in a mad rush, before you reach out for something you think you want so much that you are willing to suffer to obtain it.' The words conveyed a desperate appeal, but warmth too, and a certain strength reached out to me.

However, till I had made the enigmatic changes, did I really want her to 'look round' again for me?

I tried to fathom her words about women who meant well and got things wrong. What had 'meaning well' signified in *this* complicated debacle? What did 'wrong' mean – wrong for whom, and in what way? I had been defeated by subtleties of emotion, of calculation, for which I was unprepared, even unaware of their presence, let alone their power. Perhaps, like Esther and for that matter Annie, I too needed to become hard and calculating. If one had to do that, the sweetness of innocence must wither and die. I hated that thought. Maybe there was no help for it? Innocence was too dangerous.

I wanted to tell my aunt not to 'look round' for me any more. How could I say it without hurting her? I must say it with care, even if it meant avoiding the simple truth, that this experience had sickened me, and I wanted to steer clear of anything remotely like it for evermore. I wrote and said I needed time to get over what had happened – close enough to the truth. She wrote back at once. I was right, but she had a duty to her dead sister to do everything she could for me. It was her duty to go on 'looking round'. I was like my Uncle Zalman, she went on to say, sensitive soul that he was, whom she had worked for and cared for all these years, even sometimes saved him from making bad mistakes. I too needed a good woman to look after me, with a good heart and a good head on her shoulders.

She added that my mother would have said the same had she lived. I looked at the last photograph I had of my mother, taken when she must have been about forty, two years before her death when I was six. I wondered if the beginnings of cancer had shown in the tight lines on her face and the weary tilt of the head, her trusting, contemplative eyes, the whole imprinted with endurance and pain and courage, so different from another picture of her as the happy young woman of about eighteen holding my sister Lilian in her arms. Yes, she *would* have said the same.

I was humbled and perplexed. Was that really all that life was about – avoiding bad mistakes, keeping one's head below the parapet as Uncle Zalman had done? Was that what Mother and Father had tried to do all the time, and everyone else? Was there nothing glorious to be attempted? At least there could be the glory of trying; and why not aim for the topmost peaks whatever the price?

Reading Aunt Rachel's crabbed hand, imagining her silently mouthing the words as she wrote, tears came – for her and Uncle Zalman and their sons, for Mother, for Father and my sisters, for all of us. She was saying that this was life's reckoning. To oppose it was futile.

Far away on the horizon of my mind I began to see that my Gorbals self and my future self – already prefigured by the turning earth – were being forced into double harness. A contrary voice urged me to believe that this was not inevitable, that I did have the power to shed the Gorbals self – and I *must* do so, for that duality threatened to make all my judgements deceive me. How could I challenge life single-mindedly with the past always at hand to nudge me away from where I wanted to go, control the shape of things that I imagined were of my own free choice – thought, emotion, promptings of desire and ambition, judgement of success or failure?

I read Esther's words of finality and farewell again and again. I wanted to believe that she had tried to fight for both of us. She had lost. We had lost. After a time I felt only compassion for her, and regret for both our sakes.

Why did I persist in believing that the spirit was free? I supposed I needed that belief, as the child needed to believe in magic – and perhaps the adult too, in that secret part of him that insisted on trying to conjure miracles. Did I really have to remind myself that it was the past, not the future, that was in control, that I would feel the Gorbals at my shoulder always, like the Hound of Heaven? Why was there a perverse comfort in that thought?

NINE

La Rue Plainte

ONE OF THE UNPALATABLE TRUTHS THE ESTHER EPISODE
brought home to me was something in myself: not only did her
parents think in money terms, but I did too, though for different
reasons. The Gorbals had taught me to look at people firstly to see
if they had money, for if they had, all choices were open to them and
they had no right to be unhappy – a simplistic but powerful view, in
keeping with much of the ethos of Red Clydeside. It was hard to
forgive people who had money and were unhappy.

Wilfred, an Oxford friend, should have been happy, for he had
unlimited money. Why, then, was he trying to drink himself to
death? Why did the emotions work for him only in crude brothel
terms, beyond which he shrank from testing himself? Something
stopped me from asking him outright – why did his money, instead
of increasing his volition, have the opposite effect, tempting him to
become more and more detached?

The Gorbals outlook would have none of that. Oxford had shown
me many others whom the Gorbals assessment did not fit, who
behaved as if certain gateways could not be opened even though
they held the key – money – in their hands. What prevented them?

Certainly I envied them, which made me more bitter still.

Like Wilfred, I had still to understand what relationships were, and what they demanded. So my choice of avatars, if that was ever free, was as random as throwing dice – seemingly with as little care for where the choice of identity might take me. In Oxford there seemed to be many people who followed their inner voices with untroubled heart. They must know the answers! How did they know?

Though the Esther attachment had blazed and faded swiftly, I had believed in it deeply. The belief had not died, only retreated into the darkness. In those that followed, I knew that I only pretended belief, that some substance was lacking, though I scourged myself when each ended, leaving behind shreds of fragrance, passion, wistfulness for the might have been. I followed the marauding demon, knowing I was both predator and victim – till one day I saw that it was self-punishment. For what sins did I seek quittance?

What was the test of success in a relationship other than continued gratification? That surely was not enough, but I had tried to think it *was* – with the uneasy feeling that I was being false to some unknown law. Alec would have said there *was* nothing more.

Yet after each experiment there was the wounding suspicion – not always felt at once – that I had killed it off wilfully, through lack of consideration or finesse, not taking enough pains.

Werner's way with women – in later years, long after the death of his wife and children – made no pretence. The quest for a fulfilling relationship, he reminded me, was spurred by the delusion that finding it was the purpose of living – which was surely claiming too much. Useful possibly, nothing higher. You lived, somehow, with it or without it.

One day, when we were both travelling to Oxford for meetings, he suggested that we visit Epstein's Lazarus sculpture in the afternoon. For each of us that powerful evocation of inner conflict – between the call of life and of death – came close to the heart. The mood chimed with mine, and we went.

Werner was still dapper in appearance, but his sparse hair was now a gleaming silver. The thin lips were sensuous as of old, but the voice had acquired a slight hardness, the old precision more emphatic.

He stood looking up at the turned head of the mighty figure and traced with lifted chin, as with an invisible pointer held high, the taut folds of the winding-sheet. Its features were in travail as it strove to be free of its cerements and return to the world. Or was it fighting *not* to?

I wondered aloud: 'I wish we could stop lacerating the spirit to discover the purpose of life! We have appetites and try to fulfil them. What else is there?' I wished I could believe my words.

He paced slowly round the figure, speaking softly: 'I used to think I knew!' He shook his head. 'To think that one's life has a special purpose is a kind of arrogance. The Almighty tells us to be fully human. That is all.'

His sombre features lit up in a shamefaced grin. 'Do you remember how people here in Oxford used to talk of the mystic wisdom of the flesh – to be in tune with it the supreme fulfilment? What a conceit that was!' He held his hand up against the light as if tracing the pattern of sinews against the brilliance. On the little finger a chased gold seal ring gleamed. He said softly: 'To caress a woman is a marvellous thing – marvellous *literally*. Ah yes – that is one certainty left. But there is an end to that too, and when that time is reached, what are we to say to the spirit beneath the silken flesh, whose voice we have refused to hear? For if we have not troubled to learn its language before, it will be too late *then*. What are we left with? That thought slams a door in one's face.'

Where was the buoyant spirit I had first met on that Oxford tennis court? And myself at that time – where was I?

I said: 'What has happened to something else – all that talk here long ago about the supreme fulfilment to be found in relationships of the spirit, valued for their own sakes? It was almost a religion.'

'A tantalising dream,' he said with a shrug. You had to give too much of yourself to make relationships work, whatever 'work' meant! Or at least bearable. 'Most people simply take from you as much as they can, especially women. They would consume you entirely if you did not keep part of yourself out of their reach.' He thought about it, and added: 'I suppose I do use some people. I ought to feel guilty. Sometimes I wish I did.' He was silent.

I thought of Wilfred again, when I first knew him all those years ago. Why had fulfilment eluded him? Yes, it had been a time when maturity was in fragile and timid progress, and the temptation to postpone choices was strong. Unlike Werner he had been at the other end of the spectrum of choice and action, of experiment, judgement, risk. How could he have tried to deny that the choices even existed, when the world beckoned so richly? Why had death beckoned more strongly still?

His bitterness seemed centred on his father's riches, which he saw as sins he himself must atone for in his father's stead. He even talked of destroying the family factories – an aim I did not take seriously, but I was never sure. When I asked him why the workers deserved to have their living destroyed in atonement for his father's riches, he looked at me in reproach; I was forcing him to examine values he did not want to recognise or feared to do so. Yet he knew his obsessional detachment for what it was, and begged me not to try to persuade him out of it.

I tried reason, the only refuge I myself possessed – but Oxford had taught me that reason without emotional blindness was not enough. That debate was endless. The homely Gorbals wisdom, on the other hand, had no time for such luxury. If you are free from fear of poverty, what took its place as the spur to action? For myself that freedom was inconceivable. For him, poverty was too nebulous a concept to be considered at all. Nor was there any answer when I asked him if his skewed view of life was a good enough reason to drink himself to death, which he was plainly doing. Even as I spoke the words, I asked myself what *could* be a good enough reason. The question was absurd. For him it did not exist.

By a strange paradox, in his poetry the detachment was absent. At its best it had a diamond precision. At those moments it was easy to forget his drinking, and the occasional boorishness that marked it. He talked of his attempts to 'transcend life' and added self-consciously: 'You see, I am admitting I never learned how to get close to life!'

That was only partly true, yet he seemed to believe it, then swung away unpredictably. I tried to shake reality into him: 'How can you transcend life when you take delight in backing away from it? Perhaps you feel you don't *need* to be touched by life, like Villiers de l'Isle Adam's conceit: "Living! We'll leave that to the servants." So how can *you* say that "ordinary" life isn't real when you know nothing about it?'

'You're wrong. I do know. I've taken girls from Dad's factories, many more than I can remember. Easy enough! And for the boss's son, easier still. Drop them a few bob and do what you like with them. Take them to a crummy hotel and bung the staff to keep their mouths shut. It's not difficult. Sometimes, after I had been with one, I went round our house without taking a bath for a day or two, smelling her sweat on me, determined they should all smell her. I literally sweated myself into the working class. How much closer could I get! You can't tell me anything about the workers.'

I marvelled that he could believe what he was saying, seeing and not seeing.

In spite of that, a jewel gleamed in him: his sensibility, even with its blind spots. Quite capable of seeing clearly, he often sheered away from the perception unless he could immediately put it into his verse, as if that placed it in a different order of truth, demanding no adjustment to absorb it. In that respect, he was the opposite of myself, for I was unhappy when I knew I was not seeing the world as it really was, a recurrent perplexity, and strove to sharpen the image if I could. I preferred *my* version of that duality.

I must have reached a crucial stage in understanding it in the summer term of 1939, in retrospect a deceptively still fragment of time when 'normality' was already slipping away, being replaced by a consuming crucible of change, the 'last days' as I was already calling them.

During the term Wilfred asked me if I would care to accompany him on a cycle tour in France in the long vacation. He knew I had never been out of the country. As I would be doing him a favour – as he tactfully put it – he would like me to come as his guest. He wanted to postpone his return to his family.

We rode along Roman roads in northern France straight as far as the eye could see, between files of poplars standing to attention in a tranquil land. Whenever I ventured to speak the French I spoke in Oxford with my French tutor, I savoured the irony of being taken for a typical Englishman. I wondered what the Gorbals would think of that! Once again, as in The Cavalier, I asked myself whether I secretly wanted to be taken for one of the boss class. This time I was not sure.

We swam in the Cher, ate and drank under spreading trees in country inn gardens, climbed the double staircase of Chambord and surveyed its lordly domain from the miniature village on its roof. We talked and talked, searching through time and illusion.

At lunch near Saumur, an Englishman in tweeds and polished brogues with a bristling military moustache, probably in his forties, came over to our table and pleasantly passed the time of day. Learning that we were going south, he lowered his voice: 'A word of friendly advice. If I were you I'd make a point of getting back to England well before the end of August. Europe's going to blow up. Take it from me. I know. I'm heading back *now*.'

This was in late June. What did he know? How did he know it?

Many of us had expected Europe's powder keg to 'go up' the previous year. Would another miracle happen to save us again? Here we were, trying to believe that dream and hope and imagination, our own private world within ourselves, were the only things of importance.

We watched the ramrod figure stride away, get into a large Rover saloon and drive off, heading north. His oracular words had wrenched our thoughts to an eerie halt. Here, enclosed by trees and flowers and sun-dappled stone houses, where a few moments before we had felt joined to the slow pace of a seemingly untroubled land, the whole world was erased, and all speculation was folly. Why had we taken the man's words so readily to heart? Only then did the real present return, the worrying *zeitgeist*, the signs and portents of unthinkable calamities impending, potent resonances that put the whole of life in doubt, which we had thought we could shut away.

We tried to resume our deep-flowing talk but its freedom had gone. An unidentifiable fear, a new awareness of enveloping fate, replaced it. All time, present and future, was now conditional. The random character of his visitation had given it an apocalyptic force impossible to dismiss.

He had endowed the future with fabulous inevitability, the kind that encourages extreme behaviour – when the wheel has turned and cannot be turned back. We tried to forget about him. But the next day the effect of his words remained as if he had only just spoken. For no obvious reason, our nerves were drawn tight. That might have prompted us to the strangely automatic behaviour of that day.

Arrived in a sleepy little town, Wilfred said: 'I'm restless. I need some excitement. Let's find somewhere where there's music and gaiety.' We stood in a deserted little square in the golden sunshine of late afternoon, the hour when we usually paused to think of where to stay for the night, where to have a drink and food – healthily tired from the day's mileage. Instead we felt dissatisfied, incomplete. A middle-aged man walked meditatively on the shaded side of the square, hands behind his back. Wilfred asked him where we could find music and gaiety. The man winked and said: 'Rue Sainte – number 50. You will find what you want there.' He gave us directions, then turned away and resumed his pacing.

Wheeling our cycles, repeating his directions to ourselves, we were soon lost in a maze of winding narrow streets shaded from the sun by dun-coloured houses leaning together, asleep in this quiet time of the summer day. There were few people about, and those we asked for help shrugged and turned away. We began to wonder whether our informant had taken a rise out of two gullible young Englishmen in baggy cycling shorts. The name of the street he had given – Rue Sainte – began to sound dubious. In another quiet square we put the question, with all the innocence we could muster, to a girl of about seventeen in a pale-blue dress with white collar, carrying a leather attaché case, who might have been on her way home from school. She stared at our baggy shorts, blushed and looked quickly away, and seemed about to flee. I had begun to guess what 'Rue Sainte number 50' was. Plainly this girl *knew*. An odd thought struck me: the whole population knew, and watched us from behind closed curtains, enjoying our discomfiture.

She must have decided at once not to claim ignorance, but simply to tell us what we wanted to know and go on her way. There was no Rue Sainte, she said. Someone had been mischievous. It was the Rue Plainte we wanted. Breathlessly she gave us detailed directions and hastened away, shoes clacking dramatically in the sleepy air.

Number 50, a solid stone house like the others in the little street, proclaimed correctness with closely drawn white curtains. As we leaned our cycles against its front wall no sound came from within. Wilfred raised the massive iron door knocker shaped like a huge fist, and let it fall in a double knock. A door opened in the depths of the house, followed by a short burst of song and tinny music before it slammed shut, then quick footsteps approached. We heard bolts drawn behind the front door, which was opened by a woman in her forties, in a tight black satin dress, dark hair pulled back from her brow. A careful smile of welcome changed to a frown as she noted our shorts. She made to close the door, saying firmly: 'You must be mistaken . . .'

Wilfred, with silken, quick-witted charm, said that her house had been recommended to us as the best in the region and we could not possibly think of going to any other. She smiled to herself, then stood aside and motioned to us to enter quickly, closed the door and bolted it, and led us along a corridor to the back of the house where another heavy door gave on to a large room furnished as a bar, with small round tables lit by hanging paper lanterns. In a corner, stairs led up to a floor above. From a gramophone at one end of the bar counter came the thin Italianate voice of Tino Rossi singing *'Dans la nuit, écoutez les mandolines'*. Women with soldier companions, and a few men on their own, sat at tables round an open space and watched a young woman, naked to the waist, dance with a dishevelled soldier in dark-blue trousers with a white stripe down the leg seams, obviously very drunk, who either did not notice that his trousers were open under his belt or knew the exhibition was part of the establishment's provocative entertainment. In a little enclosure beneath the stairs lurked a group of women heavily made up, blouses hanging open and skirts gaping, obviously part of the 'stock', waiting for trade.

I had half-expected something like this when Wilfred had talked of music and gaiety; I knew he had been an experienced brothel client since his sixth-form days. The reality prompted me to retreat. A trivial circumstance made me stay. Wilfred was crossing the room to where the 'stock' waited. The young women eyed his approach narrowly, shook blouses away from shoulders, made encouraging gestures, moved a little apart from each other, a seemingly carefree but watchful business response. I would have liked to let him know that I was leaving and would wait for him outside, but I could hardly interrupt his progress now. I decided to wait at an empty table near the door.

He quickly made his selection, then led the laughing woman to the stairs, and pushed her up before him, holding her from behind.

I thought of Kirstie and Jeanie in the Saltmarket, and their show of warmth contrasted with this tawdry gaiety. I changed my mind and got up to go – I would wait outside beside the bicycles.

Before I could move away, Madame stood before me, holding by the hand two women from the 'stock', both now bare to the waist, nudged them towards me and left without a word. The women, looking practical and shrewd and amused, took post on either side of me. My shorts attracted their hands and they took possession and pressed close and with that contact I was lost. Their intoxicating body vapour enveloped me and completed their dominion.

They spoke as one: 'Your little trousers are so charming! *Oh là là* – your need is great!' They leaned across me to exchange a whisper, and one of them laughed and was gone. The other took my hand to a firm breast and said: 'Now you have chosen! We go – yes!'

Holding me, she led me up the stairs, silent now, presumably having decided that sham gaiety was inappropriate. At the top of the stairs she removed her hand – the rite must not be over too soon.

Her narrow room was papered with a trellis pattern of tea roses; it was just wide enough to hold a black iron bedstead against one wall – with a single sheet tucked tightly under a thin mattress – and against the other a washstand with enamelled basin and jug of water, a small chest of drawers on which stood a photograph of a little boy of about three, and a thick lighted candle in a brass candlestick before a coloured picture of the Virgin in a gilt frame. At the end of the room, a cane chair stood under a narrow casement window. She stepped out of her skirt and stood naked before me, and recited a bill of sale – a few coins for the linen, another few for *le pauvre enfant* – 'My penance, you understand?' – and the fee for the celebration itself. All must be paid at once. That done, she briskly drew my clothes off and put them on the chair and washed me, the water ice cold. Was that to slow down urgency? I was ashamed to be standing before her in naked appeal, to receive the detached ministration of those knowing fingers. None of this was what I wanted, or rather part of it was, but it ought to be happening in conditions quite different, with a special celebrant, my unique fulfilment. I cursed myself for being here in this decent woman's cell.

I wondered if she guessed these thoughts, and whether they mattered to her. She bent over and dried me carefully, her face tilted downwards in ageless complicity. My eye traced the little ripples that ran down her spine as she moved, the line of her neck where the dark hair parted. What were her thoughts? Would she tell me if I asked? I tried to think of the subtleties of the question in French, while she turned to the wash-basin and stood with legs apart and methodically washed herself in the same water.

I stopped trying to frame the question when she stood up straight in the narrow space between wash-stand and bed, and seemed to wait for a movement from me, then brushed closely past me face to face and paused again – and I saw, too late, that she expected me to take her in my arms; as I hesitated, she sat on the bed and stretched out, hands by her sides, looking up at me. With a little murmur she reached out to my hips and drew me down on to her and whispered, not recognisable words but surges of breathing that sounded like words, a whisper and a movement, another whisper and a movement, and another – hypnotic mantras. I was transported away, and it seemed that I stood apart and watched the figures on the bed, she managing the rite from beneath, the celebrant lapped upon her as on the slow waves of a rolling sea. And then lay motionless on her, cast up on the shore.

There came a long low murmur of tenderness from her, and I was filled with guilt. Then after some moments of silence she moved from under me and stood up and washed herself once more, and it seemed that this time she took longer about it. In some way it must be part of the enactment. She turned to face me and smoothed her palms down her supple flanks, gave a little shrug and reached both hands to my loins and held me in a show of homage, then pulled me slowly off the bed and washed me, also in the same water, again with more ceremony than before. I wished I could say something, if only to tell her I was grateful. But I felt a traitor to her because I could not believe in her tenderness.

This was a temple of detachment, not redeemed by the benevolence, almost divorced from money, that Kirstie and Jeanie in the Saltmarket had offered. How could I expect it in this place? The woman seemed to sympathise, as if she said: 'You must not expect more! No – not here!' Our roles were unalterably separate. Again I wondered if she understood. Perhaps she did. Perhaps it was her job to understand.

She went to the chair and picked up her blue skirt and turned to face me as she stepped into it, a smile on her sallow, southern features, buttoning the waist band, leaving the flared material to gape in front. The skirt was not for modesty; it was part of the play. 'Do not worry,' she said. 'You are strong. You will come back and I will teach you more. It will be so. I know it.'

Feeling clumsy, I dressed. She led me downstairs, where she gave Madame some money and whispered in her ear, pressed my hand and moved away to rejoin the 'stock' under the stairs. Madame looked at me enigmatically, but with a hint of sympathy, and led me to the table I had occupied before, brought me a glass of Pernod and moved away without a word.

The girl with the drunken soldier sat on his knee nearby, her hand on him, trying to raise his interest, either to prove that she was earning her money before ministering to him in private or to entertain the congregation further. His head lolled on her shoulder, eyes unfocused. His flesh moved in her hand and subsided. Intently, she hitched her skirt up till she was bare from the waist down, and turned towards him to make contact. His flesh rose a little further, bringing a round of applause. She called to a woman from the 'stock' to help her, who shrugged off her open blouse before she crossed the floor. The two women led him sprawling out of the room through a door behind the bar.

I wished I could see into the girl's mind. Here was detachment too. This was a stage, her proud deportment, taut young breasts quivering with the movement of thigh muscles, disciplined to the part. This was not a place to come to for sentiment.

I had lost track of time when Wilfred came down the stairs and crossed the room to join me. Business-like, he drew a line under the experience. It had been 'nothing special', he said, and questioned me closely about mine, every movement, every position, before announcing his heroic tally. I gave a truthful answer. He looked at me as if he heard a dangerous heresy that questioned his faith. I did not admit that I had thought of backing away from consummation, but he probably guessed.

Madame accompanied us to the street door and with canny courtesy invited us to return the following evening, when she would arrange an entertainment that would make us feel at home. What could 'at home' mean in that place, I wondered. Could she have in mind a variation on the girl and the soldier, a performance that had spoken eloquently of life and faith and death? As if she intuited the thought, with an unexpected flourish she spoke of 'expressions of the body and the soul . . .'

Thinking our separate thoughts we found rooms for the night, and adjourned to the garden of a neighbouring restaurant for supper. The sun had set, and the velvet darkness suited our mood. Wilfred said: 'The way you behaved in that place, you won't learn much about life. You've got to do more than dip your toe in it!' The image brought an apologetic smile to his broad face.

He added: 'You have to give yourself to everything with no holding back.'

Did he know he was repeating my judgment on *him*? I said: 'If *that's* what you call giving! You've done plenty of it through the years. And how much further on are you?'

He threw his head back and looked up through the foliage that hung over us like dark lace against the stars. At last he looked down, chastened: 'To tell you the truth, I don't know.'

I thought of that soldier's condition. Was unconsciousness the only respite from the world – and mere living not enough? *The Ballad of Kirriemuir* came to mind, and the woman's cry for someone to take the place of the swain who was spent – and all the others round her who had gone before him:

> 'Phall [who'll] dae it this time,
> Phall dae it noo?
> The yin that did it last time,
> Cannae dae it noo!'

I saw her supine on a grassy bank, and clustered round her the disconsolate youths – for what was left to them all in that moment but mere living? And that was too terrible to be borne.

I wanted to tell Wilfred that in his obsession with sensation he was trying to believe that the soul did not exist, or, if it did, that its demands were invincible riddles, best left unheard. From that state the only refuge was inner silence, a kind of death.

I did not see that I was identifying in him defects of my own. How often do we do that?

I could not know that he had only twenty years to live. He remained isolated even after he married, a match made for him not long after this journey. He wrote less and less, and in what he did write he showed increasing detachment – that dark impasse of the enchained spirit. Perhaps the Medusa blocked his vision by asking him: 'What do you want to do with life? Tell me if you dare!'

I knew her glacial stare. I too waited for magic to set me free, as he probably did, though he would never have admitted it. If I had known that so many years would pass before Jacqueline appeared, I too might have lost hope. Perhaps no woman had pointed the way for him simply by being there, or he had not been ready when it *had* happened.

Looking back, I see that my concern for Wilfred reflected fears of my own. He carried the Furies on his back and he knew it. If I helped him placate them, perhaps I would escape them too? While he shrank from accepting his visions and acting upon them, turning away from reality, I played a different version of the same game. I persisted in doubting the value of what I achieved, and trapped myself in false modesty. Only long afterwards did I allow myself to see that since leaving the Gorbals I had often pursued the appearance and not the substance, in things and people – the outsider's self-wounding mistake.

Playing the outsider had doubtless begun in the Gorbals, the lonely child hoping for comfort, believing that the 'others' were at one with their condition and owed him something on that account. At Oxford, a true outsider, I may have knowingly played the role in the beginning – perhaps overplayed it sometimes – as a drawing-room joke, the Gorbals boy 'fitting in'. But I might have overplayed it in another sense, shutting people out. No wonder relationships foundered, if they started at all. I forced people to make a greater effort to move towards me than I was willing to make to reach out to *them*. Many must have suspected the truth long before I myself did, and turned away hurt, unable or unwilling to tell me why. Who is generous enough – or has patience enough – to advise you to offer real instead of counterfeit emotion?

For a long time I told myself it was not my fault, but that of 'the others' for not being generous enough to conquer my defences – or of the Gorbals, my Medusa.

Wilfred must have decided that Oxford had given me nothing more than surface sophistication; and that the Gorbals was the true heart of me. How that perception had come to him was mystifying, for he knew nothing of the Gorbals – it was not even a place to him, only a distant name. But I did see the truth at last, that detachment was a refuge for me too. Instead of preaching to him, I must find a cure of my own.

Decades later I was still trying to fuse my new clay with the old Gorbals firing, to make good what was gone for ever – wasted time.

I had tried to silence one voice in particular, the most important and the most poignant: that of my Gorbals familiar, the shade I had left standing on the pavement outside the tenement when I pushed away on my bike for the first ride to Oxford. I imagined I was shedding him as one sheds a garment that no longer fits – refusing to see that he fitted me as nothing else ever would, that he *was* my true self. In him I tried to dismiss the world I desperately wanted to leave behind, lest it cloud my vision with misleading intimations from the past – for the past was surely bad because it *was* the past. I was too green to separate the good which the past contained, the truth, from the rest. For years I refused to believe that I would never comprehend the new world correctly – and myself within it – without him. Besides, to delete part of oneself was impossible. And for as long as I attempted it I would be unsure *who* I was, like Hoffman without his reflection in the mirror.

They were costly years – before I grasped how wounding it was to try to see the world and myself clearly with two images of them superimposed; and yet not completely, more often drifting apart, the 'true' face always in the background pleading for acceptance.

An old belief persisted from childhood, that a new version of myself would one day replace the old one entirely, the most important victory I would ever know. But my familiar knew this was fantasy, and I knew that he knew – and that he would never stop entreating me to see it for what it was.

Wilfred must have sensed this duel with my familiar when he said: 'You have to dive in – holding nothing back!'

But *how* it was to be done was not then clear. We were very young, younger perhaps than we should have been, too young to know that time was without mercy.

We made the deadly mistake of believing that only the immediate was real, the only thing one could be sure of, a finite statement to which alone we could respond – and all else was conditional and malleable. Perhaps at the back of our minds we continued to hear the warning words of that soldierly Englishman, with the feeling that there was *no* view of the future that we could trust. And yet we insisted that there *must* be.

In our separate ways we had spoken with greater knowledge of ourselves than we perceived – and shrank from it, insisting that all was not yet written, the future still waiting to be shaped.

Twenty years later he would show me that the visit to the house in the Rue Plainte, and the self-examination it had prompted, had dug deeply into him.

He told me so indirectly, and alas too late, at least for himself. He died suddenly, and not long afterwards I received a sealed envelope he had put aside, addressed to me and stamped ready for posting. *When* he had left it to be sent to me, I could not discover, but I felt it had been done recently. In it was a single sheet of paper on which he had written, in his neat square handwriting, four lines that might have been the beginning of a confessional meditation; it was saddening to sense in them an emotional turning of neglected inner pages so long after it might have saved him:

> *Winds of inveterate guilt*
> *Question the restless temper,*
> *With dreams of exiled summer,*
> *In the Rue Plainte.*

I wished I could conjure what he would have added – or perhaps he had written more, and had destroyed it. He must have known that these words would speak powerfully to me. They brought bitter regret, for his sake and mine, for time thrown away — which was perhaps why he had not sent them to me earlier — and remorse for his own lost days, and vicariously for mine. He was right about the inveterate guilt. I did feel guilty for so much done wrongly or too late — but especially at that moment because I felt I had come off better than he had, for at least I still had life. Perhaps he had had a premonition, even at the Rue Plainte, that his time would be short. There was no one I dared ask; and even if there were, what good would it do now? As for my coming off better than he, it was a presumptuous fancy — and even if true, was it to my credit or the luck of the draw?

Yes, the Rue Plainte was well named. Its impressions returned again and again as if designed by divine irony to reiterate what damage wilful ignorance could do. Those lines spoke to me with a potent innocence, clung to so painfully for so long and to such tragic purpose. They spoke for both of us.

TEN

Troy

IN A DOVE GREY ROOM IN THE MUSEUM ON THE GREEK ISLAND, shafts of late summer sun slanted down through tall windows like buttresses of solid gold guarding the Marine Venus standing in sinuous pose on a plinth in a corner. Our group from the cruise ship gathered before it.

For me, Venus had never been a romantic or sympathetic being, but rather remote, a symbol of passive acceptance of life, indifferent to values except those of expediency and passion. Her seeming serenity was suspect, and beneath it was turbulence, waywardness; and finally there was the decadence of the Roman world view. Here in this remote chamber she prompted obdurate questions of ends and means, of the springs of life, and challenged the reasons for this particular journey.

I was transported to a different statue, a homily in rougher stone, the Lazarus in Oxford – last seen with Werner – to the torturing doubts on the stone features, and questions I had not been ready to see at the time. Now, I thought I *was* ready.

Werner had talked of being consumed by relationships, especially with women, and keeping his distance in protection. His words had struck me as grossly insensitive from him of all people; for the Lazarus spoke of much more, of being consumed by the world. Wilfred had understood too well that people consumed each other simply by living – and necessarily so; but would not accept that this was only a partial statement of the human condition. It occurred to me, standing in this Venus sanctuary, that both points of view sprang not from fear of life but a desire to embrace it fully. It was because I now understood this that I was standing here.

Werner's words, I had supposed, had been prompted by a new awareness of his age; he was about fifteen years older than me. Changes in him, not noticed in earlier years, were more disturbing than I had expected, and I felt the deprivation that comes when links with a valued friend – of understanding, of response to the world – can no longer be relied upon. He no longer thought of a new relationship with the delight of former days, but paused first to weigh the likely pleasure against the probable burdens. How could he of all people, who had shone as a paragon of courage and humanity and curiosity, retreat from discovery – about himself, others, life?

At the back of the room a woman's voice broke the respectful silence, calling to the guide: 'Can you explain something I have always wondered about – why did the sculptors in ancient times make their statues without arms?'

Genteel surprise rippled through the group. Did the others recall childhood days when they too had pondered that question? I thought back to the time when I had first sensed, half in fear, half in exhilaration, the wild cries of the ancient world – rage of conquest, sack of cities – when I must have intuited that statuary, expressing as it did a people's world view, seldom escaped the victors' frenzy.

Our guide, an elegant woman dressed in light grey that blended with that of the room, wearing her silver hair in coils like a coronet, stood with casual grace beside the marble figure, her head just above the level of its slender waist. She pointed up to an inclined marble shoulder: 'Oh no – they really didn't. See – look where her arm was broken off.'

The woman persisted: 'But the armpits, I mean where the arms should be, they are so smooth, I thought . . .'

The guide shook her head gently. 'You must remember this. She lay for many centuries in the sea. Look! See where the movement of the waves and the sand smoothed the marble where the arm broke off – perhaps she was thrown into the sea when the city was sacked or, who knows, fell off a ship in the harbour.'

The questioner sighed and seemed satisfied, as much perhaps by the sympathy as the answer.

For me a vast door into the past had been thrown open and a great clamour of voices surged in. I was in another museum, in Glasgow long ago, when I was about eleven, and still saw history as magical theatre.

On a school drawing expedition, I had gone for the first time to Kelvingrove Museum and Art Gallery, a few minutes' walk from the Mitchell Library. In a long glass case raised on slender legs of fluted mahogany, something drew me with magnetic power. It was a frieze of warriors in greaves and chest armour and plumed helmets, swords raised over fallen men, and women bent down low in lamentation. Glasgow and the Gorbals were spirited away as if they had never been. Exhilarated and fearful, I was in another world. The scene was alive before me, far away and yet close, and I was in its midst. It receded from me only when the art mistress appeared at my side and persuaded me to join the rest of the class and collect my sheet of drawing paper for the morning's practical session. After that day, I went to the gallery whenever I could and stood before the frieze till every detail was engraved on my mind.

I was seized by a new awareness, of an age-old purpose to life, and of myself as part of it. Before that day, history had been a sequence of battles in which kings and heroes challenged destiny, and magic decided the result. I now saw the conflicts as between real people, though mysteriously some of them were gods or allied with gods, a distinction that never stood still. Looking at the frieze, or even when I thought about it, I felt the world shake under iron tread, heard clash of weapons, cries of fury and savagery, triumph and defiance, and the wind of death. Although elements of magic remained, the gods obeyed rules not very different from those that governed men and women. They were creatures of light and shade, of mood and sensation, always mutable, and though they could wield immense power they could be vulnerable. I was being thrust forward by Destiny, suddenly aware of new and challenging meanings in everyday things, which I must quickly absorb and act upon, but with the uneasy feeling that I would never be sure that I did so correctly. For what was 'correct' would be in constant flux as everything else would be.

That frieze told me that it held the secret of life, but what it was I must discover for myself. As in a new awakening, I began to see myself for the first time as a distinct individual, and each person as unique and separate. And I asked myself unfamiliar questions. What did people *mean* – in themselves? What was their purpose, for themselves and each other? Did each *have* a separate purpose?

Teachers told us that the frieze conjured scenes from the Trojan War, touched upon at that time in school lessons – stories of Odysseus and Achilles, Hector and Paris and Helen and the Immortals. Why did a special magic flow from Troy? Why had the Trojan War lasted ten years? Some hidden element in the way Troy was spoken of marked it as a titanic hinge-post of history. What was the secret of its enduring power?

Why the Trojan War had happened was far from clear; the story of Helen and Paris was not convincing – at that young age the force of passion did not have the required impact on the imagination. The fables recounted in lessons revealed little of the forces underlying them, which in itself was frightening. Were they so terrible that the teachers dared not tell us about them?

Schliemann's name surfaced in my reading in the Mitchell Library. A vast canvas unfolded, a palimpsest of mythic influences, passion and ambition, power and greed, envy and fury and fear. Without understanding why, it struck me that Troy and the Trojan War must have conditioned the way people thought and felt and behaved ever since, in a continuous flow of belief and purpose that must still resonate around me even in the Gorbals! From those distant whisperings the Gorbals had made *me*.

Troy haunted my sleep. Stretching back beyond the power of the Gorbals lay Troy and the heroes. I imagined myself going there to look for answers, to stand in the ruins of King Priam's halls, and let the earth under my feet answer my questions.

I knew it would be a long time before the dream would be realised. In the mirage of time, somehow I would find the way.

The more I read, the more Troy's mystery and grandeur increased. As with other miraculous events that stood out mightily in legend and Scripture – the Flood, the parting of the Red Sea for the Israelites – Troy would not be diminished by reasoning.

How could that awakening in the Kelvingrove Museum have buried itself so deeply that it might never have happened, only to stir again a lifetime further along the road?

There had been many times over the years when I could have made this particular journey. Perhaps I had feared to conjure that early revelation again, which I now saw reached back to my distant forbears, sages and priests – the *cohanim* – and paid tribute to them, and to the cast of mind they had kept alive through the millennia to pass on to me. Now, it seemed, I was ready.

How had the idea of this cruise cropped up at all, the first ever contemplated? Again, a trivial event. A friend had gone on one with his mistress of the moment, and recommended a cruise as 'worth a try when you have nothing better to do'.

'Why not?' I had said, and thought no more of it, until one day in autumn the subject of a holiday being mentioned at breakfast – we had been too busy to go away before – I put the cruise idea to Jacqueline: 'Why not?'

'Oh, yes! Ephesus, Delphi, Olympia – all those places! Why not?'

Thoughts of Troy must have played their secret part, masked in talk of organising a holiday with the least effort. That Troy was among the places to be visited was fortuitous; it happened to fit the cruise company's programme for the time of year, noted in passing: 'Ah, yes – Troy is on the list!'

There must be something destined in this trip, I admitted to myself, for intrinsically there was nothing to explain the caprice of going on a cruise at all. Troy's inclusion must have decided the matter. So Troy must be the reason for going. Why not?

As the list of site visits accomplished unwound behind us, and the ship reeled in the sea miles to Troy, the importance of that goal increased, and I wished I had gone on this exploration long before. What quittance would it bring? Would it turn over a new, blank page for me to offer up to the future, my pilgrim's prize? I only knew that my quest – the dream of that boy of eleven – had brought me to yet another critical point. How much of the old quest was still valid? It seemed that *all* of it was. I was returning to its beginnings.

A prime merit of this type of cruise, essentially a well-organised conducted tour with accompanying lecturers, was that instead of ourselves having to make the journeys between sites, our hotel, the ship, did the travelling – from one convenient mooring point to the next. Usually these journeys were done at night, to conserve the voyagers' energy and provide more time for site visits. In the past, we had travelled on our own with no set plan, mainly in Italy, often visiting the remains of Hellenic cities, Metaponto, Paestum, Elea . . . in days when their silences were not yet ravished by tourism. Books and dreams guided us well enough. We lingered undisturbed among Cyclopean shadows, and saw visions of the life that had once been lived among their certainties.

Travelling independently, we had time to reflect in peace, and allow the sense of place to touch us with its own peculiar drama. At Elea on the Salernitan coast, for instance, visited long before, when excavation had advanced only a short distance into a grassy mound facing the sea, we walked along a cobbled Hellenic street to where it disappeared into the raw wound the archaeologists had cut into the mound, and stood and imagined the rest of the street still living its old life in the darkness within. Only on *our* side of the mound, in the open air, had the living world drained the street of life. A handful of other travellers arrived while we were there. They kept their distance, doubtless cherishing dreams of their own.

Although the cruise efficiently compressed into twelve days a tally of visits that would have taken us many years in our old piecemeal fashion, there were certain inconveniences – perhaps peculiar to us, and probably inescapable in these latter days of mass tourism. When we boarded a coach at a quayside in the early morning for the dash over mountain and ravine to reach an intended site – no doubt partly an effort to get there ahead of other cruise groups, an aim seldom achieved – or jostled through crowds when we did arrive, we often thought wistfully of the leisurely days when we had wandered at our own pace, without the pressure of programme and crowds. As the distance to Troy shortened, I asked myself if the effort was worth it. It must be.

Members of our cruise were of three sorts. For one, a detached minority, the cruise might have been a distraction from other distractions. A much larger one was far from detached – 'old cruise hands', many of a certain age, in whom the ardent endeavour of younger days still burned high. On the coach returning from a site, or at table on board afterwards, eager voices sought a similar dedication sensed in others, or already known from earlier cruises: 'Seeing that gateway again, didn't it make you feel somehow . . . ?'

'How right you are! I remember it so well from the cruise before last – or was it the one before that? I couldn't wait to see it again . . .'

The third group was the largest, its members the least detached, pilgrims pure and simple, driven by a single, enigmatic purpose. Possessed by wonder that they were on the cruise at all, many spoke of it as 'the trip of a lifetime', long awaited, never to be repeated. They had saved up for years, in money and in emotion, to make this journey.

'Trip of a lifetime' could have many meanings. All of them were charged with emotion that was almost palpable, as if the whole of life had been held in suspense till now, this journey awaited in awed anticipation, its true purpose not yet understood, as perhaps it never would be. And so much was expected of it that perhaps it could never be completed.

Trying to divine their expectations was intriguing. Would it lift life up and irrevocably transform it? Was an ethereal passion stored up in preparation for a climacteric experience – whence future perspectives would be changed forever? Was the aim to find quittance for debts they owed life – or that life owed them; settlement for failed courage or faith in the past – fugitive resolve to be mourned for the last time? In one of the shattered cities we were to visit was there a message waiting, in a cypher intelligible to one voyager only at any single moment – a different message for each! No wonder the words 'trip of a lifetime' were spoken with bated breath. Some redemption, a cleansing of the soul long prayed for, waited to be won.

No wonder they were the largest group on the ship.

Was I in similar case, staking great hopes on a voyage into the interior, loaded with emotion perhaps too deeply hidden, or too long neglected, to expect quittance this late in the day? Was the trip a perverse charade, with no relevance to where I was on my journey – an excuse to go on believing that the quest could still be fruitful? I refused to accept that.

No – my purpose was valid. I must stand on windy Troy in the penetrating Hellenic light and listen to its voices, and look down into Schliemann's Trench at the cities buried one beneath the other, piled up on the wear and tear and defiant hopes of the past, a true reflection of the human condition.

Of course one thing must be true above all else. The Troy I sought was a mirror to hold up to my own past, my presence an affirmation, a bearing of witness.

At some of our stops along the way, the ship had been dwarfed at the moorings by mammoth cruise craft like floating multistorey buildings. At the Troy landfall it seemed that all the cruise ships in the world had assembled, a massive invasion fleet, to decant battalions of people seeking a foothold on Troy. Would there be room to *stand* when we got there, and peace to listen?

At the end of the bus journey, the extensive parking compound filled with ranks of coaches, it seemed that most of their passengers were ahead of us, either at the site beyond the brow of a low rise, or on their way there, or making their way back. Others, including some of our newly arrived party, milled about, some disengaging to go to the toilet huts, or to buy tourist items at a stall, or waited to be herded in the right direction. Coach windscreens bore coloured labels and numbers, and we ourselves were correspondingly labelled and numbered. Tour officials, some bearing staffs mounted with coloured identification posters, intercepted anyone without a label, or wearing one from another visit, and attached a correct one, or gave direction or reassurance to the aimless or bewildered. Shouts in various languages dominated the proceedings. Tensions filled the air, more highly charged than at any other site visit.

Beyond the compound, across a piece of open ground dotted with scrub, there stretched away a wavering column of people, or rather two columns, one aiming for the site – as yet invisible – the other making its weary way back, an endless crocodile. A few hundred yards across the plain, the outward column dissolved into a cluster of people halted near a clump of trees containing a structure whose indistinct outlines conjured an unbelievable possibility. I murmured to Jacqueline: 'Could they possibly have done it?'

'Done what?' she asked, then added quickly: 'Don't tell me they've built a wooden horse? How *could* they do such a thing!'

'I have a feeling the tourism authorities here couldn't resist the temptation.'

Excited cries floated back to us from the sizeable assembly before the structure, many of them in bulging check shirts and peaked baseball caps, spread in loose formation to aim cameras at it.

The horse was about thirty feet high, an overpowering version of a child's toy horse, a visual aid for the jaded adult imagination. It seemed to be constructed of timber, painted grey-blue with touches of gilt, the head at a jaunty angle, a broad body with a sturdy door at the side, the whole resting on stumpy legs of thick planks. We left the intense photography session and hurried on ahead – though our hopes of finding freedom to move about on the site itself were fading.

On the hill of Troy people perched uneasily, clinging to one another on every possible inch of ground, between hummocks of large rounded stones, giant pebbles polished by time, scattered over the whole area – the gathering must have numbered several thousand. New arrivals contended for space to *stand* let alone walk. Deciding not to compete for footholds on the crest of the hill, we shuffled towards a sign: SCHLIEMANN'S TRENCH. There we were trapped in a solid traffic jam, whose front rank clung precariously to the slender barrier at the edge of the Trench, while the restless crowd behind threatened to push them into it – something that must have happened before, to judge from warnings from anxious guides. We were lucky enough to be able to peer between people's heads into the long depression, like a dried-out ditch, partly filled with yet more giant pebbles.

The crowd heaved impatiently, *willed* the stones to speak, fearing to move lest a signal from the past escaped them.

Some gave up, frowning in disillusion, and fought their way from the Trench to seek enlightenment from tour guides. The babel of tongues battered the mind.

I thought of the plain we had crossed to gain this precarious foothold. Who were now the attackers and who the defenders of the citadel? Were the shades of Troy asking the same question of us? If the crowd on the hill were the attackers they were doomed to fail, not knowing what the prize was. And the shades would not reveal it. Troy was defiant still.

I contemplated the figures outlined among the great pebbles on the brow of the eminence, where sentinels of old had seen the attackers advance. On every side people stared blankly, and though the babel grew louder and louder, it seemed that a silence of even greater power enfolded us. Destiny had left them nothing to focus on. The silent cities of the Trench proclaimed their triumph – for something indefinably important was being held inviolate.

The shouting lessened and people turned and looked at their companions, and then away into the distance.

There was nothing to be done but leave. What there was to be seen was not here but within.

We fought our way out of the crowd to join the crocodile trudging down the hill and across the plain to where the coaches waited. The silence in the column was only occasionally broken by laconic exchanges. Impressions were too inadequate to be shared, at least not now, perhaps never. They were being preserved to await some inexpressible maturity of understanding – unforeseen now, awaiting its time. But no one could be sure of that.

I saw that my idle remark about the wooden horse, made before I was aware of the apocalyptic impasse on the hill of pebbles, had had more point than I had guessed. The horse was there as a sop, a morsel of 'human interest' to be set against the unfathomable testimony on the hill. At least the horse *had* something to say that was immediately understandable, a simple statement plucked out of the latter-day imagination, but almost completely irrelevant.

On our way to the incline leading down to the plain, among tufts of yellowish spiky grass holding heaps of pebbles in place, burly pilgrims in an incongruously youthful motley of denims and multi-coloured shirts draped over ample hips, jostled for standing room on the uneven slope to aim cameras in farewell. Perhaps they hoped to capture, among pictures of the tumbled pebbles and the aimless throng, ghostly intimations of the past.

Here and there 'trip of a lifetime' people looked about them with undiminished curiosity. Were they adding further touches to a portrait of themselves they had come here to complete – or simply threading this segment of the experience on to the cord of memory with the other site visits, to tell them like beads for ever? Had they too discovered that in this razor-sharp Trojan air illusion and reality continued to fight each other as in the days of the heroes?

I should have foreseen that the voices I had journeyed to hear would be silent. And yet I *had* confronted the invisible shades. I had made my own private celebration, my rite of passage long delayed. My two worlds – the Gorbals and what came after – were joined at last.

Even if the shades of Troy's buried cities *had* shown themselves, the vision would have added little to the prize I had come here to possess. The journey was the sacrificial offering – that and the prize were one and the same.

There is a persistent longing that few of us acknowledge even to ourselves – to possess once again the child's intensity and simplicity of vision, which once we took for granted. We allow ourselves to dream that it *can* be regained, and sometimes we pretend to have done it, and try hard to believe it, never convinced. Browning speaks of that fugitive sense of illumination, and the doubt that attends it:

> *Ah, did you once see Shelley plain,*
> *And did he stop and speak to you*
> *And did you speak to him again?*
> *How strange it seems . . .*

Did I see the Gorbals plain *now*?

Standing within the intangible walls of Troy, emblems of man's magical attempts to manipulate reality and defeat destiny, had added nothing to what the Gorbals had told me in childhood. The shades of this place had confirmed what I had refused to accept through the years, that the voices of the Gorbals were irrevocably part of me – Mother and Father, Aunt Rachel and Uncle Zalman and Mr Wolf; and Mary and Lilian and Esther and Annie and Alec and my familiar . . . and all the echoes joining them. I had looked for one inviolate truth to take the place of them all – and, failing to find it, told myself I 'would wait till I was ready'. What did 'ready' mean? A time when truth would be less painful to accept? No, there was a meaning that went infinitely deeper, a moment when I would place my own poetic imprint on the Gorbals, as it had done on me. Perhaps I had already done so, bit by bit, along the way, and my presence here confirmed it.

The Gorbals had never claimed that a kindlier world would ever come – only that I had better not count on it. It had said, with Mr Wolf: 'You must always give the world its due' – meaning that you must divine what it wanted, and offer it up without reserve. That was the price of living. Instead of 'the world' read destiny and the powers that controlled it, and you were back among the heroes of Troy. I had needed to wait all those years till I stood at windy Troy to give the Gorbals its due.

In my beginnings I had seen the Gorbals as my enemy. A child has no room in its heart for shades of meaning. That the Gorbals might one day become an ally had never seemed possible. In all my subsequent battles with life, I had begun to see, unwillingly, that the Gorbals had presented a rough and ready code of tolerance with which to address life. My presence here acknowledged it. I had taken the Gorbals with me after all.

When the Oxford scholarship freed me from the Gorbals, I had wanted to think it was for ever, only to be reminded again and again that the freedom was provisional, and in any case could never be complete – for wherever I went my familiar's absence tugged at my heart. Or rather his partial absence; although I had left him behind, perhaps as punishment for reminding me of a past I did not want to take with me, he had clung to me in poignant concern, refused to be shaken off altogether. His was the heroic voice demanding that I see the whole of things without evasion. Where I was tempted to leave new visions of life for another day to digest, he insisted that I see life as it was at each moment, as Sophocles did:

Who saw life steadily, and saw it whole.

I feared him for seeing too much.

When had I first seen him as a figure in the mirror standing apart from me? It must have been in the years after Mother died, when my sisters left home for ever and Father needed support in his loneliness, and I myself needed support and did not know how to ask for it. Perhaps because of that, part of me did not want to help him, and that brought guilt, though at the age of nine I did not know why I was guilty, or even what guilt *was*, a dull ache of the spirit like toothache. Guilt and inadequacy must have fought within me, and I must have realised, frightened by the sense of knowing things far beyond my comprehension of the world, that I could not help him until I knew much more than I did – a feeling made explicit much later – what I was, and why.

Did childhood magic ever triumph over the inexplicable realities of life? Only for the moment, while the spell lasted. Would the pain of unfinished business ever end? How could it, while sensibility remained?

Some Gorbals voices remained unappeased. What did appease mean? Only that history, like Troy, always renewed itself. The debts were owed to myself. How often had I wanted to look in the mirror and feel no regret? Regret was realism, recognising one's footprints in the moment one made them – or rather in the moment before – knowing they could never be erased.

I had travelled all this way to discover that Troy was a catalyst of the spirit. The journey could only continue.

Yes, I had seen the Gorbals plain.